Claiming Our Deepest Desires
The Power of an Intimate Marriage

M. Bridget Brennan
Jerome L. Shen

LITURGICAL PRESS
Collegeville, Minnesota

www.litpress.org

1	2	3	4	5	6	7	8

Library of Congress Cataloging-in-Publication Data

Brennan, M. Bridget, 1941–
    Claiming our deepest desires : the power of an intimate marriage / M. Bridget Brennan, Jerome L. Shen.
      p. cm.
    Includes bibliographical references.
    ISBN 0-8146-3012-X (pbk. : alk. paper)
    1. Marriage—Religious aspects—Christianity.   2. Intimacy (Psychology)—Religious aspects—Christianity.   3. Spiritual life—Christianity.   I. Shen, Jerome L.   II. Title.
    BV835.B675 2004
    248.8'44—dc22   2004003641

Dedication

This book is dedicated to the many people who have been our companions on our journey of married love.

- Our families who nurtured us, welcomed us, and led us to discover that there is much more about the Irish and Chinese that is similar than is different.
- John XXIII Christian Life Community who was present to us in the good times and the bad, who called us forth and freed us to discern our call to marriage.
- Tom Curry, S.J., who guided us through the prophetic discernment of marriage and who offered us a box of Kleenex as the tears of *yes* came forth.
- Our sons, Francis Xavier and John Paul, who are signs of joy of our marriage covenant.
- Sister Joan Marie Gleason, C.S.J., our spiritual director who guided us toward the life and light of love and who loved us as a mother hen loves her chicks.
- Daniel Durken, O.S.B., who called forth this book from our hearts and our minds.
- Len Kraus, S.J., and the staff at St. Francis Xavier (College) Church, St. Louis, Missouri, for their encouragement, support, and belief in our Mission.
- The many married couples we have met through our marriage ministry who confirmed our belief in the holiness and energy of marriage.

From the east to the west a perfect offering will be made.
(Ps 103:12)

Contents

Introduction

A. Purpose of this book

Writing this book will help us grow in love and intimacy. We want to live what we write. In working out our conflicting, different, and even similar views of life and relationship, we hope to forge a greater unity and intimacy. We trust this process will infuse our writing with the total energy of our experiences rather than just the intellectual learnings that are devoid of life's experiences. We hope that in the process we will express our love for each other and our belief and trust in the God of love.

Our friends and colleagues have encouraged us to write this little volume. Through our studies (mostly Bridget's), our reflections on our experience, and insights from friends and faith groups, we have come to a greater understanding and appreciation of relationship. We have shared our reflections with others in retreats and seminars. Many of those who have heard us find what we have to share helpful and resonant with their own experiences. Encouraged by those responses, we want to present our story to a larger audience.

We discuss the spirituality of marriage to help married couples realize that they are already living spiritual lives. We refer to the documents of Vatican II to let married couples recognize that they are implementing the prophetic vision of Vatican II. Our purpose is to affirm and inspire couples to live their marriage covenant.

But most of all, we write this book in gratitude to God for the gift of relationship. It is our hope that these pages will help you, the reader, gain a greater appreciation of your relationships and experience the joy that God has promised us who love.

B. What we believe (spirituality of marriage)

A number of central beliefs constitute the spiritual foundation of all that we say in this book. We have learned these tenets from our faith in Jesus Christ and have found them to be true in our own experience. God gives us the gift of intimacy and calls us to relationship; Jesus reveals himself to us in our human loving; and the Holy Spirit leads us to love's perfection in heaven. Love, intimacy, and relationship will not be possible if we do not have faith in God.

We believe that we are created in relationship and for relationship. We are created in relationship with God, our Creator, with our fellow human beings, and with all of nature. We find our identity when we discover our relationship with God, with our fellow human beings, and with nature. We are created for relationship with all those who touch us and are touched by us. In relationship, we experience both the joys and the sorrows of love and intimacy.

We believe that relationship is a gift from God. Most specifically, Jesus revealed this gift to us at the Last Supper (John 17). The gift of relationship is given so that the purpose of creation may be accomplished—that we come to know God's love for us. Relationship is a gift from God so that we experience both God's love and complete joy.

We come to know God through relationship with other persons. In marriage our spouse is that specific other person with whom we grow in love and intimacy. "If anyone says, 'I love God' but hates his brother, he is a liar; for whoever does not love a brother whom he has seen cannot love God whom he has not seen" (1 John 4:20).

We grow to love, to be intimate, to know each other through our experiences. Our experiences are total experiences: intellectual, emotional, physical, and spiritual. We grow and learn from our experiences when we are aware of them and understand and accept their meaning. For a married couple, those experiences are not only a life lived together, but also individual experiences that are shared with each other. When we share experiences, we enter into each other's individual experiences. Life is the total summation of our experiences. The meaning of life is the meaning of our experiences.

We believe that relationship is worthwhile in and of itself. Although love for one another is most often expressed in being and doing for each other, love and intimacy are much more than that. The essence of a relationship is the gift of myself to another and is worthwhile even if we do nothing for each other; it is unconditional.

We believe that joy, sorrow, peace, and happiness are fruits of good relationships.

Joy is an experience. It is the experience of love and intimacy, of the goodness of my beloved, of my own goodness because I am loved. My joy is complete when I can experience the moment of intimacy and at that same time understand, appreciate, and accept its meaning. My joy is diminished when I cannot enter fully into the moment. I may not recognize someone's love for me. I may doubt my lover's intentions or reject the intimacy out of fear. I can feel myself unworthy of being loved. Rembrandt's painting *Return of the Prodigal Son* evokes a moment of great joy when all doubts of contrition and forgiveness are laid aside in the face of the great love and intimacy expressed by the embrace of the father and son.

Sorrow is also a fruit of relationship. There is no sorrow or pain for the loss of loved ones or for breaks in relationships if there is not love in the relationship. We cannot be hurt if we do not risk relationship. Nor can we experience love and joy if we do not risk relationship. The depth of our sorrow reveals the depth of our love. Relationship does not end in death but continues and reaches its perfection in heaven. Thus, sorrow is temporary and turns into joy when the perfection of relationship is achieved.

Peace and happiness are fruits of good relationships. Peace comes from knowing my relationships and understanding that they are secure and will last. If I can fully trust my relationships, then I can be at peace, even in the midst of turmoil. I have no fear because I know love will conquer all.

Happiness results from the experience of joy. It is not simply the satisfaction of our expectations or needs. We often find happiness when we do not expect it. Sometimes we are disappointed by that which we think will make us happy, and are pleasantly surprised by that which we do not expect. Therefore, rather than seek peace and happiness, seek to build relationships of love and intimacy. For peace and happiness are fruits of good relationships. Instead of asking what will make us happy, we can ask, "How can we grow in love and intimacy?"

We believe that God calls us to relationship and makes it possible for us to love and become intimate. God has planted in our very being an inner desire to love and be loved, a yearning for relationship and intimacy that is the core and foundation of our being. As William Barry puts it, it is "the desire for only God knows what—a desire that will be only satisfied in God."[1]

This desire is actualized in our realization of the experience of love. C. S. Lewis describes such an experience as "surprised by joy . . . an experience that had taken only a moment of time but which made everything else that had ever happened to me seem insignificant in comparison."[2] Barry describes such an experience as a desire for relation-

---

[1] William Barry, *Finding God in All Things* (Notre Dame, Ind.: Ave Maria Press, 1991) ch. 2.

[2] C. S. Lewis, *Surprised by Joy: The Shape of My Early Life* (London: Geoffrey Bles, 1955) 22. This is quoted in Barry, *Finding God.*

ship and union. Such an experience also brings a sense of wellbeing and of being desired by another.[3]

For many reasons we do not often recognize or accept the call to relationship or have the courage and generosity to accept the call. But God continually sends people into our lives to awaken that desire and to empower us to answer the call. As Len Kraus, our pastor, reminded us, God never gives up on us. God calls us even unto the very last moment of our lives and does not accept no for an answer unless it is our last irrevocable no. Our personal conversion stories and that of many others attest to the truth of this belief.

The crucial fears that keep us from knowing love and intimacy and God are

- Can I trust the intentions of the lover, and
- Can I trust that I am lovable?

Can I trust God and my human lover to love me personally and unconditionally? Or must I earn that love? Can I trust that my desire for love and intimacy will be satisfied in relationship? Or am I being misled by that desire into opening myself up for rejection and pain? Am I lovable for myself? Or am I that ugly person that no one can or will love?

We all want to know that we are lovable and that we can trust both God's love and human love. Yet, our fear of a possible no keeps us from risking a relationship. Fear of a no prompts us to construct reasons for not asking those questions. If we do not ask the questions by risking the relationship, we can avoid getting a negative response. But if we do not risk relationship, we can never get the yes that we desire.

Relationship is a journey of redemption that frees us to let go of those fears that hinder intimacy, growth, and trust in

[3] Barry, 37.

God. When we let go of our fears, we gain the courage to follow our inner desire for intimacy. When we take the risk to enter into relationship, we ask the crucial questions. As we experience affirmative answers to these questions, our trust in God, in our lover, and in ourselves grows, and we are able to risk more to grow in intimacy. Our growth and redemption continue until we can abandon all fears, doubts, and self-centeredness that prevent us from (giving and receiving) unconditional love. Then we are ready to enter heaven and enjoy the perfection of relationship. Then our joy will be complete and we will receive the eternal Yes that satisfies our entire being.

As Dick Wesley asserts in his book *Redemptive Intimacy,* we are redeemed by intimacy. For it is the overwhelming joy of our experiences of intimacy and love that deepens our desire for relationship, gives us the courage and generosity to change, and empowers us with the hope and trust to persevere to the perfection of love.[4]

We have learned these beliefs from our faith in God and have found them to be true in our own experiences. It is very encouraging to us that others before us and with us have also found these truths through their experiences.

We also realize that there is a possibility we may be wrong. Certainly there are many who do not believe as we do. However, if we cannot trust our own experiences, what hope do we have for the fulfillment of our deepest desires? If God is not to be trusted, there will be no hope for us and we will be the most abject of creatures, totally unable to experience joy and happiness.

But we are not wrong. We have experienced great joy in relationship. And in this book we hope to present reflections that may help you discover more fully these truths in your own experience.

---

[4] Dick Wesley, *Redemptive Intimacy* (Mystic, Conn.: Twenty-Third Publications, 1985) 109.

Having summarized our beliefs on the spirituality of marriage, we remind the reader that a spirituality that is not relevant to practical living and that does not express itself in concrete positive actions and choices cannot yield fruit. If our spirituality does not affect how we live, then it is of no use to us. We find that many who do not actively practice their faith still believe in God.

In a practical sense, spirituality is experiencing God's presence and actions in our lives and accepting and cooperating with God's actions. Spirituality that is learned from our total experience of mind, heart, emotion, and spirit is the most affective and effective. If spirituality is only in the mind, it does not result in actions. It is no more than theology or philosophy. For many years I, Jerry, knew spirituality only in my mind. My pious thoughts were consoling for a while and led to many good intentions that were never carried out. It was not until I fell in love with Bridget that I experienced true love and recognized that others loved me. It was the transforming experience of love that gave me the desire, courage, and generosity to act on my good intentions. Experiencing love with one's entire being always leads to positive concrete actions.

Spirituality that is devoid of positive action cannot yield fruit. Our desire for intimacy and relationship will wane in the face of our fears, our frustrations, our self-centeredness, and our other desires. We will lose sight of our goal of relationship and drift apart. Without God, we can not sustain positive, concrete actions over a long time.

Therefore, in the following pages we propose an integration of the spiritual and the practical aspects of marriage. Our experience is that this integration takes place gradually. As the two of us grow to become one, so it seems our individual lives become more integrated. We will try to deal with the necessary practical aspects while always focusing on the essential spiritual facets of marriage.

C. The exercises and reflections

Our hope is that this book will inspire readers to reflect and discover the truth for themselves. For this purpose we have added exercises and reflection questions at the end of each chapter. We realize that some of the questions are difficult and risk vulnerability. Therefore, we suggest the readers do only those exercises they feel comfortable with and are capable of doing. For those who prefer writing, we recommend that you keep journals of your reflections.

1

Call to Marriage

A. God calls us to relationship

In marriage, God calls the husband and wife to relationship. God created each of us *for* relationship and *in* relationship.

> The LORD God said: "It is not good for the man to be alone. I will make a suitable partner for him." So the LORD God formed out of the ground various wild animals and various birds of the air, and he brought them to the man to see what he would call them; whatever the man called each of them would be its name. The man gave names to all the cattle, all the birds of the air, and all the wild animals; but none proved to be the suitable partner for the man. So the LORD God cast a deep sleep on the man, and while he was asleep, he took out one of his ribs and closed up its place with flesh. The LORD God then built up into a woman the rib that he had taken from the man. When he brought her to the man, the man said:
>
> "This one, at last, is bone of my bones
>   and flesh of my flesh;
> This one shall be called 'woman,'
>   for out of 'her man' this one has been taken."
>
> That is why a man leaves his father and mother and clings to his wife, and the two of them become one body. (Gen 2:18-24)

Thus, at the very beginning—at the creation—there is the first falling in love and the first marriage.

God creates each of us and calls us to relationship. For only through relationship can we experience the love of

God for us. Throughout the New Testament and especially at the Last Supper, Jesus reveals to us that we are called to a relationship of love and intimacy. In his last discourse to us Jesus gives us the gift to be one.

> "I pray not only for them, but also for those who will be-
> lieve in me through their word, so that they may all be
> one, as you, Father, are in me and I in you, that they also
> may be in us, that the world may believe that you sent me.
> And I have given them the glory you gave me, so that they
> may be one, as we are one, I in them and you in me, that
> they may be brought to perfection as one, that the world
> may know that you sent me, and that you loved them even
> as you loved me." (John 17:20-23)

The perfection of relationship is total unity with each other, with the Trinity, and with all of creation. We are to be as intimate as the Trinity, three persons in one God. God is to be in us and we are to be in God. There is no greater intimacy. We are to love as God loves: with an infinite and totally unconditional love. There is no greater love than God's love. God gave his only begotten Son to redeem us.

The experience of this great love and intimacy is the glory of God, the glory from God that Jesus gives to us. God's glory is manifested not only in great power, eternal omnipresence, creation, or the number of believers, but in God's infinite love. Through love and intimacy, God is re-vealed to us. God gives us the desire for love, the freedom to choose love, and the ability to love and be intimate. To experience love and intimacy is to experience great joy and God's glory.

> "As the Father loves me,
> so I also love you.
> Remain in my love.
> If you keep my commandments,
> you will remain in my love,
> just as I have kept my Father's commandments
>   and remain in his love.

> I have told you this
> so that my joy might be in you
> and your joy might be complete.
> This is my commandment:
> love one another
> as I love you." (John 15:9-12)

The gift of oneness is given so that the world will come to know God, and Jesus who is sent by God. Knowledge of myself, of my spouse, of my loved ones, and of my God comes through the experience of intimacy. The knowledge we gain from experience is total knowledge—intellectual, emotional, physical, and spiritual. In marriage, God's love is revealed to the world through the mutual love of the spouses. It is said in the Acts of the Apostles, "See how they love each other."

B. Call to holiness

The call to love and intimacy is a call to holiness and mission. At the Second Vatican Council (1962–1965) the council Fathers, inspired by the Spirit, wrote: "The Church, whose mystery is set forth by this sacred Council, is held, as a matter of faith, to be unfailingly holy. . . . Therefore all in the Church, whether they belong to the hierarchy or are cared for by it, are called to holiness."[1]

All life is holy. We discover God; we come upon God in our lived reality. Whatever that lived reality is—parent, single, married, religious—God is in us, and we are in God. There is still present in our Church today the concept that we praise and serve God better as vowed religious than as laity. This concept is not true, for God calls all of us to be holy and to serve, whether lay or religious. We praise and honor God when we are true to who we are. We

---

[1] Austin Flannery, O.P., *Vatican Council II: Lumen Gentium* (Northport, N.Y.: Costello, 1980) par. 39.

are holy not because of our vocation but because of who we are. The stumbling block is that we do not recognize our holiness because we do not know who we are. Anthony de Mello often used the term, "sleepwalking." We are sleepwalking through life, which is why we do not find God in our lived reality. We do not find our true self either. Not only have we lost God, we have lost our *self.*

At various times in our lives, all of us search for our true identities. Yet, often we look in the wrong places. Thomas Keating, in his book *The Human Condition*, tells the story of a Sufi Master who lost the key to his house and is outside looking for it in the grass. Some of his disciples come along and help him look for the key that he may regain entrance to his home. After a while one of the disciples asks the Master if he knows where he lost the key. Yes, he lost it in the house. But he is looking for the key outside because there is more light outside than in the house.[2] Like the Sufi Master, in our sleepwalking state, we look for God and for our self where there is more outside light (in our activities and accomplishments) rather than risk looking within where the key to holiness dwells.

Holiness is a gift given to us if we but cooperate with God's grace. It is simply an awareness of who we are, of where God is in our lives, and of how we see God working in our lives. It is so simple that we miss it. Too often we live our lives with a misinformed notion of holiness and discount the holiness that truly permeates our lives. In so many ordinary ways we live holy lives:

- The continual dying to self that growing in intimacy with our spouse demands
- The dying to self that caring for a loved one requires
- The commitment to share our resources, our time, talent, and treasure

---

[2] Thomas Keating, *The Human Condition* (New York: Paulist Press, 1999) 8.

- The call to integrity and generosity in a world of broken promises and reneged contracts.

Holiness is inviting God into our lives and desiring God to permeate our lives. "Authentic married love is caught up into divine love and is directed and enriched by the redemptive power of Christ and the salvific action of the Church. . . . Spouses are penetrated with the spirit of Christ and their whole life is suffused by faith, hope, and charity; thus they increasingly further their own perfection and their mutual sanctification; and, together, they render glory to God."[3]

C. Call to serve (mission)

By the gifts of the Spirit we are made able and ready to assume the various tasks and offices needed to renew and strengthen the Church. As it is written, "To each individual the manifestation of the Spirit is given for some benefit" (1 Cor 12:7). "Whether these charisms be very remarkable or more simple and widely diffused, they are to be received with thanksgiving and consolation, since they are fitting and useful for the needs of the Church."[4]

Holiness is not a solitary experience. If holiness is the awareness of the presence of God within us, then, by its very nature holiness moves us out of our selves. Formed in the Spirit of Christ and grounded in the unconditional love of our spouse, we are invited by God to be instruments of God's gifts—joy, compassion, love, authenticity, integrity, and thoughtfulness. We are each called to be God's presence to those who are a part of our lives.

In baptism we put on Christ and are commissioned to go forth and live prophetic lives of ministry. Our marriage

[3] Austin Flannery, O.P., *Vatican Council II: Gaudium et Spes* (Northport, N.Y.: Costello, 1980) par. 48.

[4] Austin Flannery, O.P., *Vatican Council II: Lumen Gentium* (Northport, N.Y.: Costello, 1980) par. 12.

vows are an extension of our baptismal vows. It is in the sacrament of marriage that we live out our baptismal promises. It is in our married life that we actualize and make real our baptismal vows. Simply put, mission is letting go of our own egoism and agenda and entering into the Incarnation of God. God-with-us/we-with-others.

D. Marriage as covenant

Marriage is both covenant and contract. We know that now. However, church history reminds us that marriage for many decades was viewed as a juridical contract. With the writing of the encyclical *Casta Connubi* in 1930 the concept of mutual love entered into the understanding and the expectation of the sacrament of marriage more prominently. Building on this encyclical of Pius XI, the Vatican II documents, especially *Lumen Gentium*, elevated the promise of mutual love to the sanctity of covenant. The marriage between a man and a woman is a prophetic symbol of the covenant love between God and God's people.

Shifting from a contractual concept of marriage to one of covenant is no small task. Contracts can be negotiated, can be amended, and can be challenged. Covenant—steadfast love—is written in and on our hearts. "I will be your God and you shall be my people" (Jer 7:23).

Covenant is forever. In his book *Marriage and Sacrament*, Michael Lawler says: "In marriage, a man and a woman covenant to unite not only their bodies but also their persons. Marriage is for the good of persons, not for the good of bodies."[5]

The marriage covenant is both practical and ideal. It is a vision of the ideal that is realized in our attending to and carrying out the necessary practical tasks (the contractual

---

[5] Michael Lawler, *Marriage and Sacrament* (Collegeville: Liturgical Press, 1993) 22.

pieces) of the marriage. It is inspiring to speak of the lofty ideals of the marriage covenant, but unless we attend to the nitty-gritty tasks, we risk losing the covenant. This is especially true for women. Many women have been heard to say, "Spare me the ideal, help with the dishes and throw in a load of laundry." In order to maintain and grow in the mutuality of desire and the transformation of our lives in love, we need to attend to the details of life at home. Thus, marriage is both covenant and contract. The covenant sets forth the prophetic vision and motivates us to do all that is necessary to grow in love and intimacy. Doing the contractual tasks of marriage leads to the fulfillment of the covenant.

E. Marriage as sacrament

Marriage is also a sacrament. The matrimonial covenant, by which a man and a woman establish between themselves a partnership of the whole of life, is by its nature ordered toward the good of the spouses and the procreation and education of offspring. This covenant between baptized persons has been raised by Christ the Lord to the dignity of a sacrament.[6] Man and woman have been created in the image of God, who is Love. Thus, the fundamental vocation of each woman and man is to love. Since God created man and woman in love, the mutual love between a man and a woman becomes an image of the absolute and unfailing love of God for humankind.[7] As long as there is one couple on this earth who remains in God's love, God will be revealed; for God is Love, and we who abide in love abide in God and God in us (see 1 John 4:16).

Sacraments are an outward expression of an inner reality. In marriage, the outward expression of the spouses' love for

---

[6] Flannery, O.P., *Gaudium et Spes*, par. 48.

[7] John Paul II, *Catechism of the Catholic Church* (Boston: Pauline Books and Media, 1994) par. 1604.

one another is but a reflection of the deep and abiding love God has for us. God calls us to marriage. We are invited to mirror the covenant love of God with humankind. The celebration of sacrament is an affirmation of that reality.

Sacraments are not isolated, individual acts. We gather in community to celebrate the sacraments—baptism, Eucharist, reconciliation, confirmation, marriage, anointing of the sick, and holy orders. Sometimes we forget the importance of the communal element of sacrament. Not only do we need to be with others to celebrate wonder and mystery in all the sacraments, we need the support, encouragement, and affirmation of our faith community to live out the sacraments. When we gather to celebrate the sacrament of marriage, we proclaim the wonder and joy of God's unique love for this couple and for each of us.

Marriage is the tangible sign of God's presence among us, tangible in the love that we witness in a couple's love for one another. Marriage is a billboard advertising God's presence in our world through our love for one another. "Married couples should regard it as their proper mission to transmit human life and to educate their children; they should realize that they are thereby cooperating with the love of God the Creator and are in a special sense, its interpreters."[8]

Authentic married love is caught up into divine love and is directed and enriched by the redemptive power of Christ and the salvific action of the Church, with the result that the spouses are effectively led to God and are helped and strengthened in their lofty role as fathers and mothers. The intimate union of marriage as a mutual giving of two persons and the good of the children demands total fidelity from the spouses and requires an unbreakable unity between them.[9]

[8] Flannery, O.P., *Gaudium et Spes*, par. 50.
[9] Ibid., par. 48.

In *Familiaris Consortio*, John Paul II reminds us that "The sacrament of marriage is the specific source and original means of sanctification for Christian married couples and families."[10] "By virtue of the sacramentality of their marriage, spouses are bound to one another in the most profoundly indissoluble manner. Their belonging to each other is the real representation, by means of the sacramental sign, of the very relationship of Christ with the Church."[11] "To the extent in which the Christian family accepts the Gospel and matures in faith, it becomes an evangelizing community."[12]

The Christian family today has a special vocation to witness to the paschal covenant, the certainty of the hope for which it must give an account: "The Christian family loudly proclaims both the present virtues of the Kingdom of God and the hope of a blessed life to come."[13] Marriage, thus, is an eschatological event, a prophetic symbol of what is yet to be. The spouses' love for each other is but a foreshadowing of the love and intimacy dwelling in the Trinity and to which we are invited to share.

In summary, we have explored the call to marriage from different perspectives to show the richness and expansiveness of the call. But the essential truth is that marriage is a gift given to us so that we can become one with each other and with God so that we may enter into God's joy and glory.

F. Recognizing the call: mutuality of desire

To partake of the sacrament, we must first recognize and then accept the call. We do this by getting in touch with

---

[10] John Paul II, *Familiaris Consortio* (Boston: Pauline Books and Media, 1981) par. 56.

[11] Ibid., par. 13.

[12] Ibid., par. 52.

[13] Ibid.

the deepest desire of our being. God's call to relationship is a desire planted in our inmost being. At the beginning of our being we experience a desire to love and to be loved, to be united with our loved ones, and to belong and to know our rightful relation to others. Babies develop better physically, mentally, and emotionally when they are held and loved by their parents. Children seek to be loved and accepted by their peers as well as their parents. Teenagers, by their behavior, question whether they are lovable. All of us want to be loved for who we are and not only for what we do or what we have.

This desire to be loved is the deepest foundation and mystery of our being. Although we experience this deep desire, we cannot define what will satisfy it. In his book *Letting God Come Close,* William Barry says, "God arouses in us a desire for I know not what—a desire that is satisfied only when we rest in God. This is desire for the mystery of relationship that is fulfilled only in its perfection, relationship with God."[14]

In marriage we recognize this deep desire through the process of courtship and falling in love. The first step in courtship is a willingness to risk vulnerability. When asking a person for a date, we risk the possibility of rejection. We are putting ourselves on the line and asking the question, "Am I lovable? Am I lovable to someone I want to love?" There are many who do not date seriously because they cannot risk rejection.

For many years I, Jerry, was one of those persons. Asking a woman for a date was very difficult. I had to consult with my best male friend to get enough courage to ask Bridget for our first date. I was so sure she would say no. I was joyfully surprised when she took a chance and said yes. We went to the best restaurant in town and that was the beginning of our falling in love.

---

[14] William A. Barry, S.J., *Letting God Come Close* (Chicago: Loyola Press, 2001) 31.

Falling in love is the process of recognizing and expressing mutual desires. Courtship begins with some recognition of these desires. We find some characteristics of our intended lover to be attractive. These may include physical beauty, intellectual prowess, congeniality, sincerity, honesty, sense of humor, and common interests. From this limited start, courtship can lead to greater awareness of mutual desires. But a relationship can become painful if the desires are ambivalent or incompatible. We all know it is very painful to end a relationship when one spouse does not want to continue but the other does.

The crucial experience of falling in love is the unconditional love for the beloved and the beloved's unconditional love for the lover. It is a mutual experience of the goodness and beauty of the beloved. Such an experience brings about a desire to behold and to be united with the beloved. The desire is not for selfish gain or for what the beloved can do for the lover, but it is a most unselfish desire to be for and with the beloved.

Great joy is experienced when a couple comes to realize, accept, and communicate their mutual desire to love each other. This is the joy that leads to marriage. It is celebrated in literature and in song. It is the culmination of falling in love.

In summary, the essential requirement of falling in love is the mutual desire to love each other unconditionally. The essential requirement of lasting and fruitful relationships is true love. There are certainly other requirements such as compatibility, freedom from addictions and impediments, and trust. But if the love is pure and strong, it is possible with the grace of God, support of the community, and professional help, to work out some of the other necessary issues. If there is not mutual love in the marriage, there is no chance for lasting intimacy, no matter how compatible the lovers are.

G. Responding to the call

If recognizing the call is the first step to relationship, responding to that call then follows. Falling in love does not necessarily result in a committed relationship (marriage). Jesus said, "Many are called but few are chosen."

When we are confronted with the experience of true goodness and joy, we have a natural tendency to withdraw out of fear: fear that we are unworthy of such great love, fear that we are unable to make and keep a commitment to love and to be intimate, fear of revealing ourselves in intimacy, or fear of letting go of the obstacles to intimacy. The Bible gives many examples of this reaction.

> After [Jesus] had finished speaking, he said to Simon, "Put out into deep water and lower your nets for a catch." Simon said in reply, "Master, we have worked hard all night and have caught nothing, but at your command I will lower the nets." When they had done this, they caught a great number of fish and their nets were tearing. They signaled to their partners in the other boat to come to help them. They came and filled both boats so that they were in danger of sinking. When Simon Peter saw this, he fell at the knees of Jesus and said: "Depart from me, Lord, for I am a sinful man." (Luke 5:4-8)

Bridget and I visited our friend and spiritual guide when we were seriously considering marriage. Right after we made the decision to marry, I experienced a great crippling fear: "what have I done?" I was afraid of not being able to live the commitment to love and to be intimate. I was afraid of failure. Bridget also had fears. We did not talk about them at that time. Yet, like Peter, we overcame our fears and committed ourselves to each other in marriage. Our hopes for the future and our trust in each other and in God certainly eased our fears. The realization that marriage is not only for us but for the entire community of God also helped. The ultimate experience was one of joy.

Because Bridget and I loved each other so much and found our relationship to be so joyful, we felt marriage was the right choice. Our fears were inconsequential to the magnitude of the call to love and to be intimate. The experience of unconditional love gave us courage, desire, the generosity to let go of our fears, and trust in each other and in God. As a result, we answered yes to the call and committed ourselves to the covenant and sacrament of marriage. Is not this the story for all of us who freely choose marriage?

Freedom to choose

Marriage is a commitment freely chosen by both parties. Limitations on our ability to freely choose will compromise the quality of our commitment. Such limitations are often the grounds for annulment. Thus, before we can enter into marriage, we need the freedom to choose and this requires a healthy self-concept. I need to know that I can live on my own without being dependent on another. Being dependent on my spouse does not make for a healthy marriage. A healthy marriage requires two consenting, independent adults.

Fears and needs also limit my freedom to choose. If I am afraid to live alone I may marry just to alleviate my fear and not because I love my spouse. Those entering into a second marriage must complete their grieving and let go of the former spouse before remarrying. Otherwise they will marry again simply to replace their former spouse and not out of true love for the new spouse. Fear of abandonment, failure, and intimacy can limit my freedom to choose.

Addictions to drugs or alcohol and inordinate self-centered desires for money, power, success, and sex can reduce my freedom to commit myself to love and intimacy with my spouse. Unconsciously, these desires can control my actions and choices. Even my parents' addictions can have a lasting impact on my actions if I am not aware of and acknowledge the addictive behavior.

Reflecting on my own marriage, I realized that I had freely chosen to marry Bridget. I knew that I could live a meaningful life as a single person and I did not choose marriage out of need or out of fear. I married Bridget because I loved her and because I looked forward to the promise of greater good and joy.

Commitment to the covenant frees us to trust and risk.

We risk vulnerability when we choose marriage. For we commit ourselves to love and to be intimate for the rest of our lives. Some couples who are reluctant to take this risk live together for a time as a trial marriage. But the concept of a trial marriage is false. Studies show that the marriages of couples who live together for a long time before they marry are less successful than marriages of those who do not live together before they are united in marriage.

Trial marriages do not work because the commitment to the covenant of marriage is essential. The marriage covenant frees us to trust and risk vulnerability. Our actions and choices after the commitment will be different than those before the commitment. With the assurance of the covenant, we can trust each other and risk vulnerability. I can love and reveal myself to my spouse without fear of rejection and with the trust that my spouse will love me in return. Before the commitment we would be trying to please our beloved, and we would not risk anything that would make us vulnerable to rejection. In such cases, we will always doubt the true love of our intended spouse, and our actions will reflect that doubt.

H. Why marry?

We end this chapter by asking why anyone should enter into a permanent relationship, a marriage. Why did we marry in the first place and why are we still married? Our reasons reflect our desires. And our desires will impact all aspects of our marriage. Our reasons for marriage will determine the person we choose, our expectations and hopes for the marriage, our satisfaction with the marriage, and our choices and actions in the relationship.

People marry for many different reasons. If I marry for money, I will choose someone who is wealthy or who has a high earning power. I will be disappointed if we do not amass a great fortune. Similarly, if I marry for status, security, physical attraction, sexual gratification, or for personal needs, I will be dissatisfied with the marriage if my expectations are not met. Yet, if I marry to fulfill these desires, I will be disappointed even if my expectations are met. Money, power, security, or personal gratification will not satisfy my deepest longing to love and be loved. Only love and intimacy will satisfy my desire. Therefore, marrying for love and intimacy is the only reason that will bring satisfaction, fulfillment, and long-lasting joy.

Yet, I must admit that at the time Bridget and I decided to marry, I was not totally clear about why I chose marriage. The desire for love and intimacy was certainly there and that was the primary reason. Both of us wanted to respond to God's call. But there were also other reasons. All reasons for marriage need not be perfectly pure and unselfish or totally mutual at the time of marriage. It is enough that we start with the mutual desire to love each other. As we have gained trust in each other our reasons for marriage have grown less selfish and more mutual. The vision of marriage has become clearer for us and has affected its redemptive power in our lives.

I. Exercises and reflections

Reflect on the questions in each of the following topics and share your answers with your spouse and/or with the group.

1. Telling our stories

The following is a group activity that works well for small groups of four to six couples. The activity asks each couple to recreate their courtship experiences and to recall their decision to marry. When we share our stories, we help each other enrich our own experiences.

- How did you and your spouse meet?
- How did you know you were right for each other?
- Did you see God in all of this?
- Looking back now, do you see how God was bringing you together?

2. Surprised by joy

The purpose of this reflection is to rediscover the joyful moments in your relationship. We remember and recreate the past, not to hold onto or live in the past, but to understand and better appreciate the present.

Think about moments of great joy that you experienced together, i.e., the moment you discovered you loved each other, the decision to marry, the resolution of a conflict. Spouses need not pick the same moment.

- What did you do in these situations? How did you think and feel? Were the feelings mutual?
- Why did you feel that way?
- Have those feelings and thoughts grown stronger or have they ebbed away?

Gospel readings on love, intimacy, and joy may be helpful:

The Return of the Prodigal Son: Luke: 15:11-32. Experience the joy of the father embracing the returning son.

Mary greets Elizabeth: Luke: 1:39-45. Experience the joy that caused "the child in my womb to leap for joy."

The Woman at the Well: John 4:1-30. Experience the woman's joy as she runs to tell the whole village of her moment of intimacy with the Lord.

3. Call to holiness and mission

Look at your marriage from the spiritual aspects of holiness and mission. This is also a good small group activity.

- What are your personal definitions of holiness and mission?
- Are you more inclined to live lives of holiness and mission because of your marriage?
- Are you now living lives of holiness and mission in your marriage?

4. Covenant and contract

Marriage is both a covenant and a contract.

- Do you see covenant and contract aspects to your marriage now? When you were first married? What are they? Are they the same now?
- Do you see the covenant and contract pieces working together to make the marriage work?

5. Answering the call

Recall the process and reasons for your decision to marry.

- Your courtship days and what you found attractive in your spouse. Are you still attracted by those qualities?
- When did you know that you were in love and how did you know it?
- Did you both know at the same time that you were in love?
- Why did you marry? Are your reasons the same as your spouse's?
- Are your reasons for marriage now the same as they were when you first decided to marry? If they are not, why the change?
- Were you hesitant in saying yes to marriage? What ultimately gave you the desire and the courage to say yes?

Scripture readings on the response of some persons who are called by God may be helpful:

> The call of Peter: Luke 5:4-8
> The call of Moses: Exod 3:7-12
> The rich young man: Mark 10:17-22

6. Hopes and dreams

Another way of looking at the mutuality of desire is to look at mutual hopes and dreams.

- What were your hopes and dreams when you married? Were they mutual?
- What are your hopes and dreams for your marriage now? Are they mutual?
- Have your hopes and dreams changed as you grew in intimacy? If so, why and how have they changed?
- Have some of your hopes and dreams come true?
- Do you trust each other and the Lord with your hopes and dreams?

2

What Is Love and Intimacy?

A. On reflection/discernment

In chapter 1 we described the essential requirements for falling in love and commitment to marriage. We recognize that we are called to relationship when we realize and accept our deepest desire to love and be loved. We gain the courage to marry our chosen spouse when we are surprised by joy in the experience of mutual love. We seal our commitment when we see the vision of a brighter future together.

But how do we know what is true, unconditional love? How do we know and accept our deepest desire? How are we surprised by joy in falling in love? How can we come to see a mutual vision? The answers to these questions are discovered through reflection over a period of time.

Reflection, often called discernment by spiritual directors, is a process whereby we discover the true meaning of our experiences. Through reflection we come to recognize and accept our deepest desire, to learn and accept who we are, and to know and appreciate our spouse. Through discernment we discover truth and find meaning for our lives. Through reflection God is revealed to us.

Reflection or discernment is a gift from God that is unique to all humans. It distinguishes humans from other living creatures. I can reflect if I have a mind that thinks, a body that senses, a heart that feels, and a spirit that yearns for the truth. Though we have the ability, many of us offer various reasons for not reflecting: "I don't have the time. I don't need to discern. I don't find it worthwhile. I don't know how to reflect. Reflection is for the mystics. Navel gazing is boring."

Although we can reflect in a yoga position, reflection is not a "navel gazing" exercise that we derogatorily associate with Eastern mystics. Although we do reflect on our own existence, reflection is not a "soul searching" exercise alone. All our experiences, both internal and external, and all our relationships give us food for thought. Discernment is not an intellectual activity alone. Being an intellectual is not a requirement and not even necessarily an asset for discernment. Reflection is not a philosophical or theological study leading to learned thoughts and insights. It is not solving our problems or planning our day, although it is often helpful in giving us the right perspective to face problems. Discernment is not brooding and feeling sorry for ourselves. It is not venting our anger and emotions, although it can help us let go of anger and hatred. Reflection is not self-affirmation, although we may find affirmation in our experiences. Discernment is not day dreaming about impossible desires but it leads us to see new possibilities.

Reflection is looking at all the data of our lives—our experiences, ourselves, our relationships, our external world, and God—and finding, understanding, and accepting the truth. It is an activity of my entire being—taking in information from my mind, my body, my heart, my will, and my soul. Discernment is seeing things clearly as they truly are and not how they appear to be on the surface. It lets us sort out the true good and the lasting values from the false and perishable values. Reflection brings us to an understanding and appreciation of those behaviors, choices, qualities, and attitudes that promote true love and intimacy; it helps us to see and let go of those tendencies that hinder intimacy. Discernment is being honest with how we really think and feel about both the good and the bad. If we are honest we will neither falsely inflate ourselves with the good nor overexaggerate the bad. Reflection lets us differentiate our deepest longing for unselfish love that brings lasting joy from selfish desires that do not satisfy.

> Discernment may be thought of as a journey through de-sires—a process whereby we move from a multitude of de-sires, or from surface desires, to our deepest desire which, as it were, contains all that is true and vital about ourselves.[1]

Reflection allows us to accept the desire for love and intimacy and to see the possibility of the fulfillment of that desire. It makes clear our own intentions and discerns the intentions of others. When a couple discovers a mutual desire to love, they discover that they have fallen in love. Through discernment they can see and accept new options as possible for them to attain. After falling in love, they can see the new possibility of the perfection of intimacy as real for them. Reflection is prayer because we seek to know God and how God is at work in our daily lives.

Discernment is affective for our lives because knowing the truth about ourselves, about our spouse, about God, and about the world around us will change our internal disposition and thereby our external behavior and choices. Our internal disposition must change if there is to be any lasting change in our external behavior.

Even though we all have the ability to reflect, some assistance, guidance, and encouragement are helpful. There are many books on the subject of reflection and discernment. St. Ignatius of Loyola's *Spiritual Exercises* is essentially an exercise of reflection.[2] Spiritual counselors and directors are excellent sources for guidance and encouragement in reflection. Professional psychologists can also

---

[1] Philip Sheldrake, S.J., *Befriending Our Desires* (Notre Dame, Ind.: Ave Maria Press, 1994) 25.

[2] David L. Fleming, S.J., *The Spiritual Exercises of St. Ignatius: A Literal Translation and a Contemporary Reading* (St. Louis, Mo.: The Institute of Jesuit Sources, 1978).

be very helpful. However, all of us can start on our own. Most of us already do it, though we may not recognize it as such. Although we generally take quiet time to reflect, reflection can be helpful in the midst of turmoil. I, Jerry, find it especially helpful to take a brief moment to get in touch with my feelings and thoughts in the midst of turmoil and crisis. A brief moment to sort out the situation and to focus on the essentials can calm me and make me more effective in responding to the crisis. But in general, we should try to establish a certain amount of time each day for quiet reflection.

A good way to start the reflection is to rid my mind of any problems I have at that particular time. If I can entrust my problems to God, I can gain the freedom to reflect. I then take a deep breath, relax, and get in tune with myself. When I am totally relaxed, I can then ask myself how I felt and thought about a particular experience. If I felt good and thought well of it, I can accept the experience and ask why and what made it good. If I feel hurt, angry, and rejected, and if I thought the experience was all wrong, I can accept that I am angry and hurt and then move on to find out why. Sometimes I am too confused to know how I feel. Acknowledging this state of mind allows me to look beyond the confusion to the cause. Some of us may be so shocked by bad experiences that we are numb to feeling and thinking. Acknowledging and accepting that we are numb is the first step to regaining our feelings and thoughts.

Knowing and accepting our feelings and thoughts is knowing more about ourselves and how we react to our situations. Getting over denial allows us to seek the reasons behind our feelings and thoughts. Knowing the causes is a key to unlocking our desires. We had a good experience because it satisfied some of our desires. We had a bad experience because our desires were not satisfied or, although achieved, proved to be unsatisfying. "We can then move from a multitude of desires, or from surface desires, to our deepest desire which, as it were, contains all that is true and vital about ourselves."[3]

If we know and accept our deepest desire, we can discern what experiences bring us to satisfying that desire and what experiences hinder that desire. We can then know and pursue the qualities of true love and intimacy and let go of the qualities that hinder intimacy.

In relationship encounters we can also reflect on the intentions behind the actions. We may feel hurt because we misinterpret the intentions of another. We may be falsely elated because we mistakenly infer another's intentions. Sorting out our own intentions and feelings allows us to better interpret another's intentions because we are freed from the bias resulting from anger and hurt. To know the true meaning of a relational experience is to know the true intentions of the persons in the relationship. Thus, through reflection we can come to realize that God's true intentions are for our good and our joy.

There are many fears and obstacles that limit our freedom to reflect. They are the same obstacles that hinder our growth in love and intimacy. (We will discuss this in chapter 3.) I may fear being unlovable and then I may not be willing or able to accept my deepest desire to love and be loved. I may remain in denial of my feelings and thoughts because of my fears. Also, I may not trust enough to let myself see and accept the true meaning of my experiences. But reflection is a growth and redemptive process whereby with time, with the grace of God, with love and trust of my spouse and community, I can gain the freedom to reflect and to accept the truth. When I can let go of my fears, I come to know the truth of my own being.

---

[3] William A. Barry, S.J., *Finding God in All Things* (Notre Dame, Ind.: Ave Maria Press, 1991) 34–35.

B. The foundational experience of love

In chapter 1, we asserted that the foundational experience of love is essential for us to both awaken to our deepest desire for love and to commit to marriage. The experience of love is foundational because it inflames our desire to love and motivates us to grow in love and intimacy. The experience of joy is a taste of the inherent goodness of love and intimacy that fires our desire for union with our beloved. Our realization and acceptance that we are loved moves us to seek greater love and intimacy.

This transforming experience of joy is impossible to describe in words alone. William Barry cites three examples from great writers who fail to find adequate words.[4]

> As I stood before a flowering current bush on a summer day, there suddenly arose in me without warning, and, as if from a depth not of years but of centuries, the memory of that earlier morning at the Old House when my brother had brought his toy garden into the nursery. It is difficult to find words strong enough for the sensation which came over me. It was a sensation, of course, of desire; but desire for what? Not certainly for a biscuit tin filled with moss, nor even (though that came into it) for my own past . . . and before I knew what I desired, the desire itself was gone, the whole glimpse withdrawn, the world turned common-place again, or only stirred by a longing for the longing that had just ceased. It had taken only a moment of time: and in a certain sense everything else that had ever happened to me was insignificant in comparison. (C. S. Lewis. *Surprised by Joy: The Shape of My Early Life* [London: Geoffrey Bles, 1955] 22)
>
> In childhood and boyhood this ecstasy overtook me when I was happy out of doors. Was I five or six? Certainly not seven. It was a morning in early summer. A silver haze shimmered and trembled over the lime trees. The air was laden with fragrance. The temperature was like a caress, I remember—I need not recall—that I climbed up a tree

---

[4] Ibid.

stump and felt suddenly immersed in Itness. I did not call it by that name. I had no need for words. It and I were one. (Bernard Berenson. *Sketch for a Self-Portrait* [Bloomington: Indiana University Press, 1958] 18)

Took my daily walk at 4 p.m. today in eighty-nine degrees of frost . . . I paused to listen to the silence . . . The day was dying, the night being born—but with great peace. Here were imponderable processes and forces of the cosmos, harmonious and soundless. Harmony, that was it. It was enough to catch that rhythm, momentarily to be myself a part of it. In that instant I could feel no doubt of my oneness with the universe. The conviction came that the rhythm was too orderly, too harmonious, too perfect to be a product of blind chance—that, therefore, there must be purpose in the whole and that we are part of that whole and not an accidental off-shoot. It was a feeling that transcended reason; that went to the heart of human despair and found it groundless. (Richard E. Byrd. *Alone* [New York: G. P. Putnam's Sons, 1938] 84–85)

We, too, have like experiences. For those of us called to marriage, we encounter great joy when we mutually realize, accept, and communicate our desire to love each other. As with the above examples, often such moments come when some past event is recreated in our reflection, and we come to understand and accept the true meaning of that experience.

Although all our personal experiences are unique, there are some common elements to this foundational experience of love:

- being loved and desiring to love in return
- union with the beloved, with God, and with all of creation
- wholeness
- a life with purpose and worthwhile living
- gratefulness
- joy

But these are not experiences we can plan for or earn through our own efforts. Love is a gift from God given by and through our beloved. Therefore, as we stated in the Introduction, C. S. Lewis describes this as being "surprised by joy"—the joy of the love experience. If we are alert and disposed to God's love, all of us will experience this gift many times in our lives.

Reflection disposes us to recognize and accept this foundational experience. It is needed for us to recognize and accept that we have fallen in love. Because we have found our deepest desire we are awake to the love that satisfies that desire. Because we have sifted out the true and lasting values from the false and fleeting ones, we are disposed to receive the love of our beloved. Because we have purified our own selfish intentions, we can recognize and accept the unselfish intentions of our beloved. Because we have found God to be trustworthy in our experience, we can trust our spouse and ourselves. We can trust that our desire to love is mutual and that we will live out our marriage vows. Because we have shared our reflections on the qualities of intimacy, we can come to a mutual understanding, desire, and appreciation of those qualities.

Because we have thought about life and its meaning, because we have felt deeply with our hearts, because we have dealt with the confusion when our minds will not agree with our hearts, because we have known we are weak and unable to carry out our good intentions, because we have suffered the sorrow of betrayal and of loss without bitterness, because we have trusted enough to risk, because we have remained constant to the covenant when we are tempted to give up, we are ready to enter into the joy and glory of God's love.

That foundational experience is the summation, the synthesis and integration of all our experiences. Indeed, the whole is greater than the sum of the parts. The foundational experience of intimacy is greater than the greatest joy of intellectual discovery, more wonderful than the physical joy of love making, better than the deepest desire of the heart, and higher than the highest vision of the spirit. It is the synthesis of all of our being and experience.

C. Qualities of love and intimacy

What should we seek? What are the qualities of love and intimacy? What do we seek in our marriage? Bridget and I have reflected and shared what we see as qualities of love and intimacy.

Mutual desire is a quality of intimacy. The desire to hold each other and be held is a longing that grows as we grow in love. The desire for union builds with every positive experience we have together. As we sort out selfish desires, our desire to love becomes more mutual and we become more satisfied with our relationship. Our desire to be together grows stronger each day.

Trust is an essential quality of a successful marriage. The trust that is needed in marriage is not the blind trust that all our impossible dreams will come true without any effort on our part. We often use such trust as an excuse for not working on dreams that we do not believe can happen for us. Trust in marriage means trusting that our mutual desire will grow and that we will both work for the vision of the perfection of the relationship. Trust in marriage means trusting God who promised the gift of union to all who desire it. Trusting in God and in each other allows us to risk vulnerability in letting go of our fears that hinder intimacy and in revealing ourselves to one another. Trust grows as we grow in love and intimacy and as we establish a long record of faithfulness to each other. Every decision to trust, no matter how small, leads to greater trust.

Honesty is a quality of intimacy that is much more than just not telling lies. Honesty is revealing the truth about myself and my intentions. To be honest, I must risk vulnerability to reveal myself and to accept my spouse's revelation.

Honesty is being true to my thoughts and feelings, neither inflating nor suppressing them. Honesty is accepting others as they are and not as I might wish them to be. Honesty leads to transparency in the marriage. Unconditional love is transparent. Jesus tells us that God is transparent.

> "I shall no longer call you slaves,
> because a slave does not know
> what his master is doing.
> I have called you friends,
> because I have told you everything
> I have heard from my Father." (John 15:15)

Fidelity, a necessary quality of intimacy, is much more than just being faithful to my spouse. Fidelity is being faithful to the covenant. When the going gets tough and the temptation to give up is great, I must remain faithful to the call and trust God and my spouse that we can and will fulfill the covenant to remain in love. If we remain faithful and persevere in hard times, God's love will ultimately bring us to the perfection of relationship.

Mother Teresa said that "God does not call us to be successful but calls us to be faithful." We are weak. Despite our good intentions and great efforts, we will at times succumb to our fears and self-centeredness, and then fail to love. We will do things that harm our relationship or even temporarily break the relationship. "The spirit is indeed willing, but the flesh is weak" (Mark 13:38).

Our God is faithful even when we are not. God forgives our sins, knowing we will sin again. Being faithful leads us to ultimate success. Failure is never final unless we choose to make it final. Even betrayal is not final unless we choose to make it so. Look at the contrasting stories of Peter and Judas who both betrayed Jesus. Peter repented and received forgiveness from Jesus and reestablished the relationship. But Judas chose to make his failure final by committing suicide. Fidelity keeps us from giving up in failure and urges us to try again. It gives us the trust that success will be achieved, that we will overcome our weaknesses with the power of God's grace, and that we will reach the perfection in relation.

Bearing each other's sorrows is also a quality of a good relationship. There is no sorrow or pain for loss of loved ones or for breaks in relationships if there is not love. We cannot be hurt nor can we experience love and joy if we do not risk relationship. The depth of our sorrow reveals the depth of our love. A great act of love and intimacy is to allow our beloved to enter into our sorrow. If we do not enter into each other's sorrows we cannot hope to enter into each other's joys. Sorrow in time ultimately turns into joy.

I, Jerry, was surprised with joy and intimacy in the midst of sorrow. After the funeral of a dear friend, I met my friend's sister for the first time in my life. As we talked about how we loved and missed my friend and her brother, a feeling of great joy and intimacy came over me. It felt like I had known this woman all my life and I wanted to share my deepest feelings with her. It was a brief conversation—not more than fifteen minutes. Yet it touched me deeply, and I will always remember that occasion even though I have not seen her since that meeting.

True love is capable of heroic sacrifices of letting go. A good example is the story of Abraham and Isaac. Isaac is God's gift to Abraham. Through Isaac God's promise to Abraham that he is to be the father of his people is to be fulfilled. But God asks Abraham to sacrifice Isaac. Abraham so trusts God that he is willing to let go of his only son. God spares Isaac and a ram is sacrificed instead. On the surface, it seems that God is testing Abraham. But God, who is all-knowing, already knows of Abraham's faith. Abraham, however, does not know how strong his faith in God is until that moment when he trusts enough to let go of his son, Isaac. God does not test Abraham's faith but, rather, God allows Abraham to experience the strength of his own faith.

The ultimate example, of course, is the story of our redemption. God so loves us that God sent the beloved Son, Jesus, to be one of us and to suffer death on the cross. Jesus so loves and trusts God that he freely lets go of his own life. We, too, are called by love to let go of all things that hinder intimacy. Ultimately we, too, will be asked to let go of our lives. If we trust in God and in each other we, too, will receive the strength to let go when our time comes.

These are some of the qualities of love and intimacy that are meaningful to our experiences. There are others such as spontaneity, openness, gratitude, generosity, forgiveness, and not harboring bitterness. Each couple can make up its own list. Because of the unique experiences of each couple, our lists may be different. But they will have common substance and spirit because the qualities of true love are universal and unchanging.

> Love is patient, love is kind.
> It is not jealous,
> [love] is not pompous, it is not inflated,
> it is not rude, it does not seek its own interest,
> it is not quick-tempered, it does not brood over injury,
> it does not rejoice over wrongdoing,
> but rejoices with the truth.
> It bears all things, believes all things,
> hopes all things, endures all things. (1 Cor 13:4-7)

Our list of the qualities of intimacy has changed as we have grown and have sorted out the true from the false qualities of intimacy. In the early years of our marriage, though we each reflected on the qualities of intimacy, we did not take the time to share our reflections. As we have become more intimate, we have found the desire to share with each other the qualities that we want in our relationship. In an exercise at the end of the chapter, we invite you to do this also.

D. Rewards of intimacy

There are other qualities that we call rewards of intimacy. These are the benefits we receive from being in love and from being intimate. Power is a reward of intimacy. The experience of intimacy gives us the power to overcome our fears, our life's trials, and our life's sorrows. We know that nothing can separate us from our spouse's love and from God's love. We know our relationship will continue and reach its perfection in heaven. No matter what the future holds, our mutual love and God's power will carry us safely through all dangers.

> Three times I begged the Lord about this,
> that it might leave me, but he said to me,
> "My grace is sufficient for you,
> for power is made perfect in weakness."
> I will rather boast most gladly of my weaknesses,
> in order that the power of Christ may dwell with me.
> (2 Cor 12:8-10)

Peace is a reward of intimacy. The experience of intimacy and love gives us a sense of wellbeing and peace. Peace comes from a realization that we have found our true desire and that our life-long search has ended. It comes from knowing that we have made the right choices and are living the life to which we are called. This realization gives us peace even in the midst of turmoil; we have found order and purpose for our lives.

I, Jerry, was given the consolation of power and peace at a recent retreat. I had just taken early retirement from my position as director of research at a leading chemical company. During the first days of the retreat, I was agonizing over my decision to retire. I sensed that I had lost the power and prestige my position and my company offered me. I no longer had access to a corporate American Express card or a corporate travel agency to plan my itinerary. My income, though more than adequate, was substantially reduced. I sensed that in the business world retired persons are less respected than employed persons. But most of all, I feared that Bridget would think less of me when I was unemployed.

I related all this turmoil to my retreat director. He suggested that I reflect on my deepest desires. At that time I did not see how his suggestion could, in any way, help ease my distress. But during reflection and prayer, I suddenly realized that my deepest desire is to love and be united with my wife, my sons, my family, and all my loved ones. I realized that power, prestige, money and intellectual ability have nothing to do with achieving my deepest desire. And I had the great consolation of God's fidelity in giving me the gift of love and intimacy with my loved ones. I am now certain that God cares for my loved ones more than I can on my own. This gift from God gave me a great sense of peace and security. I had nothing to fear. God's power is enough for me to satisfy what I truly desire. I could let go of my fears of retirement.

I confided all this to Bridget and she gave me great consolation by assuring me that she loves me for who I am and not for my position or my abilities. She said, "I will still love you even if you are totally incapacitated." She hoped that in my retirement I would find something else to engage and energize me. Two months after the retreat I found a full-time teaching position at a local university. I always wanted to teach, but there were no teaching jobs available when I had completed my doctorate. Now I thoroughly enjoy teaching and my students.

Intimacy spawns a sense of wholeness. Polly Berends in *Whole Child/Whole Parent* says, "The quest for wholeness becomes not to acquire, not to accomplish, not to complete ourselves—but rather to discover what it is with which we are one so that we can go ahead and be one with it."[5] Thus,

---

[5] Polly B. Berends, *Whole Child/Whole Parent* (New York: Harper & Row, 1987) 10.

we experience wholeness because we are one with our spouse, with our loved ones, with God, and with our universe. We are where we belong and we experience the warmth and tenderness of that belonging.

With intimacy, life will be worthwhile. For us, marriage is certainly the most difficult challenge we have ever faced, but it is also the most worthwhile. Love and intimacy give meaning and purpose to life. It is sad to see that some people who have achieved power, wealth, fame, and all kinds of material goods, are still not satisfied and find their lives to be meaningless. It is difficult to live life, but if we live for love and intimacy, then all our efforts are worthwhile and we will be satisfied.

Freedom to love unconditionally and to risk total intimacy is a reward of a perfect relationship. Only God can love unconditionally because God does not require love to satisfy selfish needs. Only the Trinity of the Creator, Son, and Holy Spirit are in perfect communion because there are no fears and obstacles that limit their intimacy. But we, as humans, have needs, fears, and obstacles that limit our freedom to enter into intimacy. If I need love out of a fear that I am not lovable for myself, I will seek love to alleviate my fears. Fears and needs can lead me to mistrust my lover's intentions, and I will see my lover's love for me as meeting my own selfish needs and not as unconditional love for my innate goodness. If I do not trust God and my spouse, I will constantly seek reassurances from them. How often do I evaluate my marriage by asking what my spouse has done for me lately? How often do I ask God for reassurances?

These questions are natural and should not cause undue concern. Love and intimacy do not start out in perfection. In marriage we begin with imperfect love and partial intimacy. Thus, we start with needs and wants that arise out of fears. There are boundaries we establish that we do not want anyone, not even our spouse, to cross. There are parts of our being that we are afraid to share, even with our spouse. There may be a fear of intimacy itself, of becoming too close. But our hope and God's promise is that we will grow to the perfection of relationship. This growth process takes time to build our trust and let go of our fears.

William Barry uses the example of scaffolding. Before we build a wall, we must build a scaffold. Once a strong wall is built, we can take down the scaffolding and the wall will stand on its own. Barry tells this story:

> A fox asks St. Exupery's little prince to be his friend. The little prince wants to know how to go about it. The fox replies: "You must be very patient. First you will sit down at a little distance from me—like that—in the grass. I shall look at you from the corner of my eye, and you will say nothing. But you sit a little closer to me everyday."
>
> The next day when the prince comes, the fox tells him: "It would be better to come back at the same hour so that I can anticipate your arrival. If you come at just any time, I shall never know at what hour my heart is to be ready to greet you. One must observe the proper rites."[6]

As we grow in love and intimacy, rites and needs diminish until we are free to love unconditionally. As we sift through our desires for love and intimacy, they become more mutual. We will be less demanding of each other because of conflicting desires. As our wounds are healed by love, we are more able to let go of our fears and those needs that come from our fears. As we gain the trust that results from a long history of fidelity, we are freer to risk vulnerability for the sake of intimacy. And when we are free to love unconditionally, we can enter into the eternal joy of the Trinity. We can pray with St. Ignatius of Loyola:

Take, O Lord, and receive my entire liberty,
my memory, my understanding and my whole will.

[6] Barry, *God's Passionate Desire and Our Response* (Notre Dame, Ind.: Ave Maria Press, 1993) 16.

All that I am and all that I possess you have given me:
I surrender it all to you to be disposed of according to your
    will.
Give me only your love and your grace;
    with these I will be rich enough, and will desire nothing
    more.

Ignatius's prayer reflects what is already true or destined to be true in our lives. God's grace is already poured for us, and we are destined to give up everything, including our bodies, when we die. What is really significant about the prayer is Ignatius's acceptance of the truth of himself. When we let go and trust in love, we become free to love unconditionally.

Finally, the greatest reward of intimacy is joy. We are created for joy, and Jesus came to give back to us the joy we lost with Adam's sin.

> As the Father loves me,
> so I also love you.
> Remain in my love.
> If you keep my commandments,
> you will remain in my love,
> just as I have kept my Father's commandments
> and remain in his love.
> I have told you this
> so that my own joy might be in you
> and your joy might be complete.
> This is my commandment:
> love one another
> as I love you. (John 15:9-12)

In our loving, we bring joy to the world and our joy will be complete.

E. Relationship is worthwhile in and of itself

When I love someone, I go out of my way to do good things for my beloved. And love certainly motivates me to do and to be for my beloved. But the essence of relationship is not what we do for each other. Relationship is worthwhile in and of itself even if the lovers do nothing for each other. This truth is revealed in the story of Job. This is the consolation Job received from God as he sat naked on his ash heap, completely stripped of all that God had given him. Job's consolation was the deep realization that although God had done nothing for him and seemingly everything against him, he still could love God. And, although Job had done nothing for God, God still loved and related to Job. Job experienced that he was lovable for himself and not for what he did to earn that love. He could love without the condition of receiving from the lover. (See Job's final answer to God, Job 42:1-6.) Relationship is worthwhile in and of itself without condition because the essential gift is myself and not what I do.

F. How do we express and receive love?

For most of us, our story is not Job's. We express love through actions and intentions. But in this imperfect world, our actions and intentions are not always clearly communicated to our beloved. Thus, it is helpful for couples to share with each other the ways that they express their love. We often do not notice, understand, or appreciate our beloved's efforts to love us. A true story that appeared in the newspapers provides a good example. "After twenty years of marriage, the husband said to his wife, 'I do not like meat loaf.' The wife, who had made meatloaf for him religiously every Sunday for twenty years, was shocked. She said, 'You loved the meatloaf that my mother made for you while we were courting.' And he replied, 'Well, I was trying to be polite.'"

Even after twenty years, it is not clear how we love each other. In marriage, we have the privilege of helping each other to love.

G. Exercises and reflections

Take a few moments to reflect on the following and then share your reflections with your spouse.

1. Qualities of Intimacy
- Identify five qualities that you most desire for your relationship? Are these qualities the same or different from your spouse's?
- What experiences have brought you lasting joy? Why?
- As you look back on your relationship, have the qualities that you desire for your relationship changed?

2. Sifting through desires
- What were your intentions, desires, and goals in the early years of your marriage? Are they the same now or have they changed?
- Were you able to sift through desires, letting go of those that hinder love and intimacy and increasing those that bring lasting joy?
- Have your desires grown more mutual?

3. Experience of love
Prayerfully read 1 John 4:7-21 and recall those you love and those who love you. Bask in the warmth and glow of love.
- What thoughts and feelings come to you?
- What gives you the desire to love?
- How do you experience that you are loved?

4. How do I love?
- How do I daily express my love for my spouse?
- How do I experience my spouse's love for me?

- What are the fears and obstacles that make it difficult or prevent me from expressing my love for my spouse?
- What are the fears and obstacles that make it difficult or prevent me from receiving love from my spouse?

5. *Trust*

- How are my spouse and I one with each other and with God? Are there patterns and themes in our relationship?
- Do I trust God? How do I trust God?
- Does God trust me?
- Do I trust my spouse? How do I trust my spouse?
- Do I trust myself?

If the answer is no, can you explain why? What healing do you need so you can trust again? Ask God and each other for that healing.

If the answer is yes, can you explain why? What qualities in your relationship lead you to trust? Ask God and each other for those qualities.

Take a moment to pray together for greater trust in God, in self, and in each other.

3

Growing in Love and Intimacy

A. Practicing love and intimacy

Growing in love and intimacy is a life-long journey of discovery, growth, understanding, and appreciation. It is choosing and living life to its fullest extent. It is experiencing the joys, sorrows, good, bad, and ordinary that life brings. It is a journey of seeking mutual hopes and dreams and taking action to actualize them. It is carrying out the marriage vows and receiving the gift of union promised by God. Guided by reflection, we sort through our conflicting desires to focus on our deepest desire to love. We come to know the true meaning of love and intimacy, and we make choices and change our behavior so as to love and grow intimate.

But how do we do all of this? The answer is that there is no magic formula for how to love. Jesus gives us examples, but he does not give us a handbook. Much is written on how to love and be intimate, yet we can only use the authors' suggestions when they are relevant to our unique experiences. Although we can gain help and insight from others, by and large we have to work out how to grow in love and intimacy by ourselves.

In a simple and profound way we can say that we grow in love by loving and we grow in intimacy by being intimate. We grow in love and intimacy by practicing love and intimacy. Every act of love leads us to greater love and makes the next act easier. Every action we take to be intimate makes us more intimate and increases our desire for intimacy. We grow and become perfect in what we practice.

B. Attitudes and disposition leading to intimacy

Though there is no magic formula, there are attitudes or dispositions that help us grow in love and intimacy. These attitudes are identified as living life as a mystery, freely risking vulnerability, and sacrificing self for the sake of love and intimacy.

Mystery: To live and cherish life as mystery

There is an old saying: "Life is a mystery to be lived and not a problem to be solved." Growing in love and intimacy will be easier if we truly believe and practice that saying. Mystery can be defined on two different levels. It can mean something unknown but knowable and solvable by human beings, such as finding the guilty party in murder mysteries or solving the mysteries of science. Given enough time and effort, we will find the answers.

On a higher level, there are mysteries that are beyond human knowledge or experience. The Trinity, three persons in one God, is such a mystery. Life, love, and intimacy are such mysteries. We seek to live, experience, and cherish the mystery of life and love, but we do not hope to understand it.

It is often easier to solve problems then to live and cherish the mystery. When Bridget seems to be upset and wants to talk with me, I often react negatively. I give the impression that I don't want to be bothered at that moment. It would be easier if I would just offer a solution so I could return to what I was doing. "Bridget, you seem down today. Why don't you go to the mall and buy that new dress you have been wanting; that will make you will feel better." My problem is solved and I can go back to watching the ballgame. But to embrace Bridget's feelings, to be with her and listen to her, takes much more effort.

Solving problems is about taking control. Living life is about letting go. I take charge in solving a problem because I want to control the process and the result. If I let go, I trust God and let God bring about a good outcome.

I pray differently when I want to be in control than when I let God be at the helm. If I want to be in control, I pray for the outcome I want. "God, give me good health and wealth." But if I trust God to be in control, I pray for God's blessing and trust that what is best for me will be given to me.

Solving problems is important. But we grow in intimacy by entering and cherishing the mystery in each other's being. It takes true wisdom to recognize the problem to be solved and the mystery to be cherished.

In a second marriage, establishing new relationships with your spouse's children and reordering old relationships with your children are necessary tasks. We can treat these tasks as problems to be solved or as mysteries to be lived and cherished.

Toward our ex in-laws, each of us would like to be able to settle our own anger or that of our spouse, to be able to forgive and to heal our hurts, but we may not be able to do this immediately. We would like to have our children accept our spouse, but this may take time. We must recognize this and be patient.

If we treat the above as problems, we will try to impose our desired outcome on them. For example, I might insist that my children accept my spouse or I might try to bribe them into this acceptance. I am really trying here to solve my own problem.

If, however, we consider the children's point of view, we can see that they, too, are experiencing loss and the fear of the unknown future. If we can give them love, support, firmness, and patience (the qualities of intimacy), they can on their own go through their grieving, come to accept the new situation, and overcome their fears. Then something really good can come out of it.

This is true in my experience with our two sons. Our older son, Francis, was a good baseball player. For three years he did very well for a select team. I looked forward to watching him play baseball throughout high school and maybe even in college. I really enjoyed watching him and I worked with him to improve his skills. But just before entering eighth grade, Francis decided to quit baseball. Surprised and somewhat disappointed by his decision, I talked with him about it and learned that he really did not enjoy playing baseball anymore. I could have lectured him on being a quitter and demanded that he continue. But I realized that if Francis was not happy playing baseball, I would not be happy either. Francis was not a quitter. He played basketball for a time and finally concentrated on track where he excelled. My letting go allowed Francis to be who he wanted to be. Giving up control is difficult, for it means we have to risk vulnerability. We cannot have closure on our timetable.

Live and cherish life as mystery, for the Trinity, love, intimacy, forgiveness, and self-sacrifice even unto death on the cross are mysteries. Certainly, this is a lesson that we have learned as a nation from the September 11 tragedy in New York.

Vulnerability

Vulnerability is a mystery. We experience vulnerability when we choose to enter into relationship. Have you ever experienced a situation in which you felt vulnerable and helpless, when you lacked control of the situation, and when you discovered your abilities were not equal to the task? In such moments, if you accept your weakness and place your trust in God, you can come to experience God.

Have you experienced vulnerability with each other? To grow in love and intimacy, I must freely risk vulnerability for I feel vulnerable when I share myself with another and allow another to touch me. I must let down my defenses to allow another to enter deeply into my being.

Some examples of when I experience vulnerability with Bridget are

- asking Bridget to respond to my needs and wants
- expressing and sharing wounds and hurts of my life
- listening freely to what Bridget has to share with me
- forgiving and asking forgiveness, taking the first step in mending the relationship.

We feel vulnerable and are reluctant to risk when we have experienced rejection and betrayal in our lives. The pains have been so great that we have reacted by building walls around our hurts. These walls close off parts of ourselves and allow us to live with the hurts. But when we are called by intimacy to enter into those walled areas, the old pains come back anew. We become reluctant to tear down the walls and risk vulnerability again. In our marriage, the covenant relationship in which God's love is poured out for us, is where we can heal those hurts and begin to tear down those walls. By our mutual love we can heal each other, drive out fear, and rebuild trust.

Freely risking vulnerability is essential to relationship. If we do not risk vulnerability we cannot discover and heal our past hurts and we cannot become intimate. Risking vulnerability is painful, but we do it for the sake of the relationship.

Self-sacrifice

Sacrificing our selfishness for the sake of union with our beloved is essential to growth in love and intimacy. Love begins with desire for the beloved that generates good intentions. But good intentions are not enough. Love must be expressed in actions. Self-sacrifice is necessary for us to love. Sifting through our desires to focus on the central desire to love requires us to give up selfish desires such as power, wealth, and pleasure. All of us who are married can recall many examples of self-sacrifice for love. At times we sacrifice our own needs when see our spouse's need to be more urgent. We let go of hurts and bruised egos when we say we are sorry and make up after conflicts. We make the sacrifice of risking vulnerability so as to become intimate.

Self-sacrifice can often be painful and unpleasant. Recently I, Jerry, had a very painful argument with my sister Betty over my assuming the responsibility of preparing my mother's house to put on the market. I felt that Betty accused me of mismanaging the work and she felt she was not appreciated by me. We parted angry and hurt. It was very difficult for me to take the first step toward reconciliation. But the pain of separation from Betty, whom I love very much, prompted me to call her to apologize. She was also ready to apologize and we reconciled with great joy.

We can make heroic sacrifices because we see and desire the goodness of relationship. We see that our self-sacrifices will ultimately result in satisfying our deepest desire. We see that the joy of intimacy is so much greater than the pain of letting go. We see the great example of our God and the Son, who suffered death on the cross for our sake. And so we grow in love and intimacy by making sacrifices.

Paschal Mystery

Making sacrifices to let go of our fears and mistrusts is a redemptive process. Through it we trust more, risk more, and grow deeper in intimacy and love. We experience the Paschal Mystery, the death and resurrection of Jesus the Lamb who is sacrificed for us so that we can be redeemed and rise with him in the resurrection.

We experience redemption through each other. God's redemptive power works through us. We heal each other of hurts that cannot otherwise be healed. Even when reconciliation and healing are impossible with the one who hurt us, our love can still give us the desire, courage, and generosity to let go and move on. For, we must let go of the past in order to live in the present and move on to the future.

Being aware of this redemptive cycle in our lives is helpful in building intimacy. We should celebrate the joy of resurrection which is always greater than the suffering of the death (letting go). These cycles are true signs that we are growing in intimacy and love.

In summary, we grow in love by loving and we grow in intimacy by being intimate. In practical terms this means that we strive daily to improve the qualities of a good relationship. And to perfect those qualities requires great trust in each other, faith in God, letting go, and freely risking vulnerability.

C. Fears and obstacles to intimacy

As there are attitudes that foster intimacy, there are also fears and obstacles to intimacy. Fears are universal to humankind. "All God's children got fears." That is the bad news. The good news is that love casts out fear. If we can own our fears and seek guidance and healing, we can move on with our lives and grow in the intimacy of God. Some fears common to all human beings include:

- rejection
- abandonment
- being controlled by another human being
- failure
- loss of spouse
- putting "me" first.

If we can be aware of our fears, we can move toward lessening them. If we do not own our fears and suppress them, we risk *not* growing in our personal relationships and intimacy. Often it is the underlying fears that are at the root of our conflicts. When we do not face our fears and suppress them, we find ourselves reacting to a present event with the pain of a past event.

Living solitary lives, we are able to ignore our fears. They are buried deep within our being. I, Bridget, believe that we are often not aware of our fears until we attempt to enter into intimacy. It is the risk of relationship and intimacy that brings our fears to the surface. There are people who would rather deny themselves relationship than risk facing their fears. Often we masquerade our fears into something totally different. I met a couple at one of our retreats who, during that weekend retreat, discussed their fears at length. The husband discovered that what he thought was compelling him to work very long hours and be away from his family for extended periods of time was his commitment to provide for his family. When his wife complained that he was seldom at home, his reply was, "I am only doing this for you and the kids." Upon further reflection he realized that it was his fear of failure that was driving him to work long hours. A common trait among people who have a fear of rejection is to over-relate with others to the point that you "have to like them" because they do so much for you. It is their fear that is driving the "doing for you," and, in time, you realize how manipulative that behavior is.

Because we risk so much vulnerability in our married lives, it is common for married couples to harbor fears they do not know about. When Jerry and I were first married, we slowly discovered that I had a fear of Jerry being possessive of me and that Jerry had a fear of being abandoned by me. Obviously, we were not dancing well! We continued to talk about the friction between us and eventually discovered the fears. What was so intriguing about these fears that each of us brought to the relationship was that they had been buried away for years, actually since our childhood. They did not resurface until we felt at some level the same vulnerability that we experienced in childhood trauma. For me it was the loss of my younger sister when I was six years old. At an unconscious level I believe my parents and older siblings "held" onto me as they worked through their grief of losing my younger sister. When Jerry and I first married I felt that he was "holding" onto me in the same way that I had experienced being "possessed" when I was six.

Jerry's fear comes from his history as an immigrant from China to this country. He, his parents, and younger sibling left Shanghai, China, amidst much chaos. They left hurriedly, under danger, with many friends and material possessions left behind. Jerry arrived here as a quiet and shy young boy, feeling very different from all his class-mates. Over the span of his teens and adult years he and his family acclimated and mainstreamed into American culture. However, when Jerry and I married, and I would have to leave for a short time, the whole experience of being abandoned returned to him. This is the mystery of vulnerability that we discover deep within our spirit, the buried moments of pain that surface. We choose to allow God's love and trust to heal that pain through the love and trust of our spouse.

About a decade ago I lost within a short span of years my remaining four siblings and my mother. My father had died earlier. Because I experienced so much physical loss within such a short time, I was very traumatized. I sought profes-sional counseling to learn how to absorb and integrate the loss within me. I was aware that if I did not face this loss I would indeed continue the pattern of my family and pass my sense of loss on to our pre-teenage sons. I chose to be honest with my spouse and sons. I explained to them that I was still emotionally feeling the trauma of loss in my life and I asked them to work with me. One simple thing I did was to ask the "Shen Men," as I affectionately call my hus-band and our sons, to call and let me know they were safe and just running late from one of the many sporting events in which they participated. My willingness to risk being honest and sharing with them my struggle and needs allowed them to choose to respect that need in me. If I had not owned my fear, the "Shen Men" would return exuberant after having won the championship, and my reaction would be, "Where the hell have you been?" Eventually, over time, I was healed of the deeper pain of loss. I still refer to my fear of loss as a "weak link" in a chain. It does not dominate my life, but it is an area of sensitivity. Occasionally the weak link gets stretched and I have to be aware of that dynamic and attend to it in a healthy manner, rather than transfer that fear onto my spouse or children.

Foundational fears

The fears that we have discussed above arise out of three foundational fears:

- I am not lovable.
- I cannot trust God.
- I cannot trust my spouse.

From the moment of our conception we experience the desire to be lovable and to be loved. Infants instinctively bond to and seek warmth and love from their mothers. Young children seek love and approval from their parents and their peers. For teenagers, love and approval from their peers seem more important than approval from their parents. We adults seek love and intimacy through adult relationships.

We can come to fear that we are not lovable if we have experienced loss, rejection, and betrayal. Since we know that love is a gift from God, we can also come to distrust God. If others have failed us, we can transfer our distrust onto our partner in marriage. These fears will prevent us from choosing love and intimacy.

But love drives out fears. Through love and intimacy, we are confronted with the goodness and fidelity of our beloved and of our God. Then we can experience with Admiral Byrd "the feeling that transcends all reason; that went to the heart of man's despair and found it groundless."

Addictions

Addictions are obstacles to intimacy. They are inordinate desires that control us. Because they control us, they limit our freedom to choose. We commonly think of addictions to alcohol and drugs. But addictions can be any behavior or desire that we cannot control. People who are addicted feel powerless to change that behavior, even when they know the consequences.

I, Jerry, have an addiction to rage. I am prone to road rage and to rage against everyone—fast food worker, airline employee, salesperson—who makes mistakes and does not show me proper respect. I remember being so angry at times that I was oblivious to the embarrassment that I inflicted on my family. I felt totally out of control. I was unable to stop until I vented my full anger. Even the threat of being arrested for public disturbance was not enough to make me stop. After the incident I would brood about getting even. I know that such behavior hurts me but for a long time I could not accept that fact and continued to justify my rage to myself. With the encouragement of Bridget and our sons, I have come to recognize my addiction. Recognition is the first step in seeking help. I have had professional help and have made progress in defusing my rage before it occurs.

My addictions can also detrimentally affect those close to me. There is well-documented evidence of the effects on children of parents who are addicted to alcohol or drugs. In fact, there are support groups for children of alcoholics. (See page 141 for resource information.) The secondary effects can be long-lasting and can limit our freedom to enter into relationship long after we have separated from our parents.

Addictions are detrimental to intimacy because they deprive us of the freedom to choose love and intimacy. But addictions, as with fears, if they are recognized and accepted, can be cured with the grace of God, support of the community, and professional help. We need not be imprisoned by our addictions. We can experience the redemption of love.

Although we are healed from our fears and addictions by love, we do not marry for the sake of healing. We marry for mutual love and mutual desire for intimacy. We seek healing for the sake of growing in love and intimacy rather than seeking intimacy for the sake of healing. If we have severe addictions and fears that impair our freedom to choose, we will need healing before we can enter into a commitment to marriage.

D. Exercises and reflections

Reflect on each of these questions and share your answers with your spouse and with the group.

1. On mystery

- Many men will say: "I do not understand my wife, but I love her." Reflect on how I see my relationship.
- What parts of my relationship are mysteries to be lived and cherished?
- What parts are problems to be solved?
- Is it difficult to make the above distinction?
- Do I agree with my spouse on the above distinctions?

2. On vulnerability

- Where and when have I experienced vulnerability (risk) with my spouse?
- How did I feel and think on those occasions?
- How did we handle and resolve these situations?
- What are some ways that we can make each other feel less vulnerable in future situations?

Suggested Scripture readings:

Two different strangers encounter Jesus. In one case the Samaritan woman (John 4:1-26) risked vulnerability and shared her life history with Jesus and was rewarded with the revelation of the Messiah. In another, the rich young man (Mark 10:17-22) wanted to draw closer to Jesus. Yet when Jesus loved him and accepted him, he walked away sad for he was not willing to risk the vulnerability of growing in intimacy. Use you own experiences to understand these different responses.

3. Paschal mystery

- All of us who are in relationship have experienced the Paschal Mystery of dying to self in order to rise as one. Recall a recent experience of dying to self and rising as one.
- What was the dying to self, the letting go?
- Was it difficult? Was the letting go necessary for greater intimacy?
- What gave me the desire and the courage to let go?
- Did I experience the joy of resurrection?

4. On fears

- Reflect on my life and our life together.
- What do I fear most today and for the future?
- How has this fear affected my behavior?
- Am I able to talk about this with my spouse or with someone else?
- Why do I have this fear?
- What can I do to let go of this fear?

Pray together for the trust and courage to let go of our fears.

5. On addictions

- What are my habits and behavior patterns?
- Are there any habits or behavior patterns that I want to change?

- Am I constantly justifying to myself why I have not changed these behavior patterns?
- Are others telling me that I have an addiction but I constantly deny it?
- Of what am I fearful?

Pray together for the trust and strength to recognize and accept my addictions, and for the courage to seek healing and professional help.

The Dynamics of Relationship

We are never right for each other all the time.
We need to keep growing and making it right.

A. Our moods and rhythms

Marriage is a dynamic living organism undergoing numerous stages, cycles, rhythms, and moods.

Despite all our efforts to be knowledgeable as we enter into marriage, we still go into the relationship at a rather superficial level which simply means that we have growth potential before us. We truly do not know ourself or our spouse as well as we think we do when we walk down the aisle.

This process of self-discovery as well as spouse-discovery is defined by marriage experts as entering into the stages and cycles of the unveiling of the marriage relationship. We are either going forward, going backward, or we have hit the cruise control button and are just going along for the ride.

The stages and cycles intersect with the various moods and rhythms of our own individual lives as well as the moods and rhythms of our lives as a couple. By rhythms, we mean the ebb and flow of a host of intangible factors that affect our view of our wellbeing, our interactions with other people, and our feelings toward the world. At times we feel good about ourselves. We are totally alert and energized, ready to take on the world. And it seems at those times the world comes to us. We hit the green at all the traffic lights. There is a parking place in front of our destination. And we find the fastest checkout line in the supermarket. At other times we feel down. We are zapped of energy and out of sorts with the world, and it seems we are constantly fighting the world. We are stopped by all the red lights. We search ten minutes for a parking space and find one three long blocks away from our destination. And there is price check ahead of us in the supermarket checkout line that we choose.

Our moods and rhythms in our relationships shift like this also. We have all experienced times when we are totally in sync as a couple. At those times both of us are excited, feel good, and are full of energy. We are eager to talk, to do things together, and to be intimate. Of course, we can also be in sync when both of us are feeling low. Then we can give each other space or try to put a little cheer into each other's life.

We have occasionally experienced times in our own marriage when our rhythms are out of sync. One of us may feel great and want to do something together. The other may be down and just wants to be left alone. It is that way when one of us returns from a trip. On occasions of reentry we are out of sync. I may return from a trip tired and wanting space alone, but Jerry is eager to have my time and attention. Or I can come home excited about reconnecting, but Jerry is preoccupied with what he is doing.

There are many elements that can impact our rhythms. Children are recognized as causing a significant shift in the rhythm of the marriage relationship. Job loss, job change, relocation, work demands, illness, death of a loved one, finances are also frequently mentioned as having serious consequences on the rhythm of a marriage.

In ordinary times we frequently discover that we as a married couple are not in rhythm. Being aware that there are rhythms and being brave enough to admit to my spouse that I sense we are out of rhythm is a first step. If we acknowledge this out-of-rhythm cycle regularly, we learn to adjust our dance (relational) steps accordingly and we will get back in step more easily.

The downfall of many couples is that they go through their marriage on cruise control or sleepwalking. They ignore the out-of-sync moments, they become oblivious to the stages and cycles, and they choose to disregard their own mood changes, but attack their spouse for his/her mood swings. If they continue to build on these negatives, they undoubtedly weaken the basis of the marriage bond and eventually there is no foundation.

All married couples face difficulties, challenges, and hard times. Why some marriages succeed and others fail is based on how the couple chooses to deal with the difficult times. If we have built up energy, affection, and attention to one another, and if we have been with one another in the good times, we will be able to be with one another in the trying times. But if we become careless during the good times, if we take each other for granted, and if we are unaware of how much effort a solid, healthy, vibrant marriage requires of us, we will not survive the hard times.

For as long as Jerry and I have been married, we have always carved out some time to talk, to share deeply, to face unpleasant issues, to seek guidance from each other, and to take classes to learn more about the necessary skills for our marriage. Each step, each effort to grow and learn has aided us in building a solid foundation for our marriage so that when we do experience difficulties, we are able to be faithful to one another and walk through the storms together.

Most couples still embark on the marriage journey believing that "all we need is love." Too many couples make the decision to marry at the infatuation stage and chemistry level, unaware that love is not all that is needed. Navigational tools of communication, conflict resolution, deep listening, willingness to admit errors and wrongdoings, a sense of humor, trust, and emotional maturity are all necessary in a good and lasting marriage.

The rhythm of our marriage dance is influenced by our moods which, of themselves, are neither good nor bad. It is what we choose to do with our moods that can be beneficial or detrimental to the marriage. We need to be aware of our moods and take ownership of them so we can then attempt to uncover why we feel irritable, annoyed, frustrated, frightened, buoyed, suspicious, uncertain, or ecstatic. It is a myth to think that my spouse can read my moods. If I can barely understand where my moods are coming from, how can I expect my spouse or anyone else to do so?

Moods influence and to some degree determine my energy level. If I am in an upbeat mood, I am ready to take on any challenge that comes my way. If I am in a negative, downside mood, I will have less energy and will begin to be impatient, curt, and surly, seeing all the negative aspects of my spouse's personality.

Our attitudes drive our moods and rhythms. We may not have control over those events that interrupt the rhythm of our married lives, but we do have control over our attitudes. My attitude determines how I respond to an unexpected job loss. I can believe "woe is me; I am doomed." Or I can feel that this is a very difficult experience but I will make the most of it, learn from it, and move on. My attitude is the mental energy that I bring to life's daily occurrences.

I, Bridget, recall when our younger son was moving into the "no" stage, with a touch of power struggle tossed in to make it more interesting. I decided I could have a win-lose attitude toward John's power struggle, or I could see beyond that slice of his developing personality and focus on his positive qualities: his welcoming smile, his warm and strong hand-holding, his creativity in the sandbox. I chose to direct my mental energy, my attitude, toward the positives in his young life, and it diminished the negatives considerably. A change in my attitude caused a positive response from my son.

B. Moods and rhythms with our extended family

The same dynamics apply to our spouse, to in-laws, outlaws, and all the characters that are a part of a marriage scenario. We can focus on the annoying habits of our in-laws or we can make an effort to search for the positive qualities. That shift will greatly influence how our relationship unfolds with our in-laws as well as our children's relationship with their grandparents, aunts, and uncles. Looking for the positive qualities in our extended family does not mean that we allow another person to treat us with disrespect or to control or manipulate us. If we are consciously aware of who we are and of what our boundaries are in relationships, then we are mature enough to maintain our own person without criticizing another. It is perplexing to hear husbands or wives continually berate their mother-in-law or father-in-law to their spouse. How can we strengthen our own marriage when we are constantly harping on the faults of the parents of our spouse? Do we really believe that continually expressing these negative attitudes is going to bring energy to our relationship?

If there are indeed glaring issues with our spouse's family of origin, our complaining about them is not going to change the problems. The only person we can change is ourselves. We do not tolerate inappropriate behavior. We make decisions so that inappropriate behavior does not touch us or touch our children. For example, if my parent or my parent-in-law watches television that we find offensive, we do not need to visit them when they watch those programs, or we do not allow our children to be there. This means I may have to find someone else to care for my children when I am away. If my parent or parent-in-law abuses alcohol or other drugs, I do not leave my children with them, and I can choose not to be with family members or friends who abuse alcohol or other substances. What most of us do is just complain about our family members and choose not to make decisions about how we need to live our lives without being pulled into inappropriate or destructive behavior. We need to distinguish between annoying behavior and destructive behavior. We can always choose to let go of annoying behavior. Sometimes we need to make very difficult decisions to assure that our children are not victims of destructive behavior.

Recently Jerry's father died very suddenly and his mother, amidst the shock and grief, became seriously ill. What this meant for me personally was that Jerry, in addition to dealing with his own grief, had to spend a great deal of time assisting his mother as she gradually adjusted to being widowed after sixty-four years of marriage. It took much of Jerry's time, which was time away from our relationship. Because I had learned to respect my in-laws and because I had a life of my own, apart from my husband, not only did I not resent the time Jerry devoted to his mother during this transition time, but I was very proud of him.

Had I not carved out a life of my own, had I resented my in-laws during the many years of our marriage, Jerry's "working overtime" with his mother would have been a good reason to be angry and resentful. Likewise, had Jerry not separated from his family of origin when he was younger, having to care now for his mother and her needs would have been one more demand on him. But this was not so because, as a young adult, he had chosen to live his own life and not allow his parents to make demands on him, while at the same time being respectful of his parents and sharing his life with them in an appropriate way.

Separating from our family of origin is considered one of the first and most important requirements in building a strong and solid marriage. Both in Genesis and in Ephesians 5 we find the mandate that we leave our parents and cling to our spouse. "That is why a man leaves his father and mother and clings to his wife, and the two of them become one body" (Gen 2:24).

While we know that we need to separate from our family of origin in a healthy way in order to establish clear boundaries, it is often difficult to do so. Some parents find it hard to let go of their offspring. Some disapprove of the person their child has chosen to marry. Some adult children are not aware that they are more invested in their family of origin than they realize. There is no scientifically proven method for separating from family of origin; often it is stressful and messy. The key is that as a married couple we create our own identity, and from that established identity we reconnect with our families of origin.

We need the support and encouragement of our families, but we also need to ensure that we keep an appropriate distance from them in order to have time as a couple to establish our own household.

C. Stages and cycles

Coupled with the various moods and rhythms of married life are stages and cycles of the marriage relationship.

First stage: bliss

The first stage that most of us recognize in a marriage is the bliss or honeymoon stage. Everything is idyllic. I have married the most wonderful person in the world. We would not risk a permanent relationship if we were not in a bliss stage. Chemistry and infatuation blend to create an illusion of the "perfect" spouse. This is not all bad. It is natural and normal. The "everything is wonderful" memory does much to move us forward during the difficult times. The fact that we can recall what we first felt for our spouse protects us through the disillusionment and power struggle stage. John Gottman of The Gottman Institute in Seattle, Washington, uses in his Love Lab the ability of the couple to recall how they met as a predictor of whether the couple will stay married. If a couple has primarily positive memories, the marriage will most likely survive. But if they remember mainly the bad experiences, the marriage is probably not going to last. This bliss stage can continue anywhere from two months to two years.

Second stage: disillusionment

The second stage or cycle is more treacherous. Numerous authors have given it various names. Power struggle, betrayal, and disappointment are a few words used to describe how we feel when we awake one morning to discover that we did not marry Prince or Princess Charming. In fact, we married someone who is pretty darn annoying! A significant number of marriages are lost in this second stage. It can, however, actually be a tremendous opportunity for growing and learning more about self and spouse.

The only person I can change is myself. However, the first person I try to change is my spouse. This won't work! I need to look at myself to see where I am in the relationship, what am I struggling with, and how I can encourage my spouse to do the same. Often at this second stage, we could benefit greatly from a third party such as a counselor to guide us, to help us sort out the feelings of betrayal and disillusionment, and to teach us skills in communicating our dissatisfaction and frustrations as well as our needs and wants. This is essential. We must learn how to deal with the conflicts and confusion that are an inevitable part of any relationship. We need to understand that living out the mystery of marriage is living out the Paschal Mystery. The dying and rising that growing in intimacy calls us to is a sharing in the dying and rising of Christ. We will emerge more freely to follow Christ in our married lives.

As the relationship unfolds, we encounter within ourselves pieces we did not even know existed. We discover fears and insecurities that, prior to risking the intimacy of love, were dormant within us. As we grow in intimacy, obstacles to that intimacy begin to evolve. We look to protect ourselves, to circumvent the vulnerability that intimacy necessarily calls forth. Once again we have the opportunity to grow and learn through this stretching. To honestly face our fears, insecurities, and anxieties, and to share this with our spouse, takes tremendous courage and energy, but is essential if we wish to continue to grow and be healed.

Our spouse's love is a critical element in our being healed of the "brokenness" within us. But first we must be willing to own our need for healing and this is difficult. There is not much in our society that encourages us to reflect within ourselves and to admit that we are broken and need to be healed.

Later stage: transformation

Reaching the stage of transformation is not a final stage. Because marriage is a living organism it continues to move through the various cycles and stages. We do, throughout our marriage journey, enter into stages of transformation where the vision of what we are called to is so clear it becomes a mountain peak experience. We all have these moments and we need them. Often following such a moment, we gradually or swiftly return to the bottom of the mountain, and here we begin again. Once more we go through the bliss to the power struggle and the disappointment only to reemerge to the transformation stage.

Each time we recycle we grow more skilled in moving through the stages, and slowly there is an intermediate stage between the disillusionment and the breathtaking transformation stage. In that intermediate stage we find ourselves resolving conflicts more quickly and with fewer battle scars. We find ourselves listening more intently and valuing our spouse's perspective. We appreciate our spouse more as gift than the adversary that we thought she or he was in the power struggle stage.

The transformation stage is very powerful in that we recognize it is through Christ, in Christ, and with Christ that our love is made whole and we are transformed. We move forward to be a sign of God's love in our world.

We live in a world that advertises the perfect myth—everything must be perfect or it is no good. A vibrant marriage allows me to demythologize the perfect myth and helps me discover that the person I married is perfect for me.

Today we live in a more isolated, non-communitarian society. It is common among married couples to believe that they are the only couple going through these cycles and stages. They erroneously believe that every other couple has it "together" and that there is something wrong with them if they are struggling. This is often a cause for divorce or, if not divorce, of great stress. Couples think there is something wrong with them because they have hit the disillusionment stage. We need to educate couples on the nature of the marriage cycle and inform them that they do not have to find their spouse "lovable" every day of the year.

What motivates us to be faithful during these various stages, cycles, moods, and rhythms of our married lives? It is God's grace expressed through the love of our spouse. We realize that the more we grow and learn about ourself and our spouse, the deeper and more profound our relationship will be. The dying of the false self allows a more graced self to evolve. As we begin to experience the occasional moments of joy from having risked and having stretched to enhance the relationship, we are energized to continue to grow. Success builds on success.

D. Needs and wants

Another component in managing the dynamics of married life is understanding that each of us has needs and wants that we bring to the marriage. In another era, couples got married and figured out what they needed to know as they went along, or they learned from their parents, something between "Father Knows Best" and "Seven Brides for Seven Brothers." It was an era when the primary focus of marriage was procreation. Everyone or almost everyone in the community shared the same expectations of married and family life, and those who did not were looked down upon. Everyone was also expected to accept a common set of needs and wants. That is both good news and bad news. The good news is that there was a common support system, a collective voice that guided the couples through marriage. The bad news is that one size does not fit all. Today we have much more freedom and individual choice. There are general guidelines set forth by our churches as well as by our society, but each couple at some level needs to put many pieces of their married life together in such a way that it is sustainable and vibrant for them. Thus, we have needs and wants that are specific and peculiar to each couple.

Requirements are the nonnegotiables in a marriage. If they are not met, the relationship will not endure. Needs are about what I must have in a relationship and not who my spouse needs to be. For example, in my marriage my requirements are fidelity, equality, mutuality, shared faith life, honesty, openness, willingness to change, emotional maturity, addiction free, and financial responsibility.

One would think that addiction free would be a given in any marriage, but consider how many people are in marriages in which there is drug, alcohol, gambling, and/or shopping addiction, to name but a few. Many young couples are in deep financial debt when they enter into marriage. Too many people rush into marriage without seriously considering what they must have for a relationship to be successful and vibrant.

We also have emotional and functional needs. Remember the tee-shirt that was popular a few years back, "If Mama ain't happy, nobody's happy," which translates "if Mama's needs are not being met, there is going to be trouble at the home ranch." Issues are unmet needs. Frequently when a couple is struggling, they can look at their needs lists and find that some that are considered necessary for a good marriage are not being met. We never get all our needs met all the time but they should be satisfied most of the time. If they are not being met, it is time to have a serious discussion with our spouse. My spouse is not responsible for knowing what my needs are nor is he responsible for meeting all my needs. I must own my needs, communicate them to my spouse and our children, and ask for help to meet them.

We have emotional needs: a warm hug, a kiss when leaving for work, expressed appreciation for my contributions to our married and family life, willingness to listen, especially when I have had a difficult day with work or children or elderly parents, time alone, time together, generosity, thoughtfulness. We all have our own list.

Functional needs are often the culprit for being angry and frustrated with one another. Some of the most common functional needs include sharing domestic chores, transporting the children to school or extracurricular activities until they are old enough to get their driver's licenses, taking accurate telephone messages, balancing the checkbook, and filling the gas tank. Each of has our own personal list that we need to share with our spouse.

Wants fit in here as well. Wants provide pleasure and enjoyment and can be satisfied more readily. Wants change over time more than do our needs. Perhaps in our younger years, wanting a bigger house or a fancier car may have been important. However, when children are added to the family, wants often switch to things more practical—a minivan instead of a two-seater sports car. Expensive clothes become less important as comfortable and relaxed attire becomes more practical when raising young children. Eating in a family restaurant is preferred to eating in a more expensive adult supper club. It is important to have wants, even if we do not always get what we want. This keeps us thinking and dreaming, especially if we can laugh about not having everything we want.

When Jerry and I moved into the minivan stage we would often laugh that we would have purchased a Rolls Royce, but we thought that a childseat would look tacky in a Rolls. If most of our emotional and functional needs are being met more often than not, we are more disposed to letting go of the wants.

We must be clear about the differentiation between requirements, needs, and wants. We must be alert to the fact that, in corporate America, wants are marketed as requirements or "must haves." This can confuse us. We must have this car, this house, this appliance; children must attend this school. This is a dangerous trap.

E. The essential and the necessary

Another distinction that is helpful in the practical living out of daily lives is that between the essential and the necessary. The essential is what is true, the essential being, and the strategic meaning and purpose. The necessary is what is needed to achieve the essential. For example, in marriage, the essential is the commitment of the couple to love, intimacy, and fidelity. The commitment of the couple to love is the true essence of marriage and defines the strategic meaning and purpose of marriage. What is necessary to achieve the strategic purpose is for the couple to love and be intimate with each other, to meet each other's needs, and to do all the other chores that keep a marriage functioning. Without the essential, there is no need to do the necessary. And if the necessary is not done, the essential will be lost.

A principle that helps us to live life is, "Do the necessary while focusing on the essential." In this way, the essential is not lost in the busyness of doing what is necessary, and the necessary is accomplished so that the essential can be achieved. Keeping focus on the essential is helpful in assigning proper priority to the necessary. After my father's death, I, Jerry, was faced with moving my mother to a new condo, selling her house, caring for her in her illness. I was totally stressed and did not know what to do. So I asked myself, "What is essential?" The answer was obvious. My mother was most important and that was the essential. So I postponed the move and selling the house so I could concentrate on tending to my mother during her illness.

F. Exercises and reflections

Reflect on each of the questions in the following sections and share your answers with your spouse and with the group.

1. Moods and rhythms
- What moods and rhythms am I in now?
- Are we aware of each other's moods and rhythms?
- Are our moods in sync now?

2. Our attitudes affect the spirit of our marriage.
- What are some of the positive attitudes that I bring to our relationship?
- What are some of the negative attitudes that I bring to our relationship?
- Can I change some of my negative attitudes?

3. *Every marriage goes through various stages and cycles.*
   - How would I describe the stages and cycles in my marriage?
   - What stage do we find ourselves in now?

4. *It is essential that we understand our requirements, needs, and wants.*
   - What do I require for our marriage to be vibrant and healthy?
   - What are my emotional and functional needs?
   - What are some of my wants?
   - Over time, have my needs and wants changed?

5

Making Decisions on Life Choices, Time, and Money

A. Making decisions as a couple

The ability to make decisions is a characteristic that differentiates human beings from other living organisms. The ability to choose is absent from lower forms of living organisms such as plants and microorganisms. They must follow the internal biochemistry of the species. Plants cannot choose where they are planted, how to grow, how or with what other plant to reproduce. There is no variation due to choice. In the higher forms of the life of animals, there is more variation due to choice. To some degree animals seem to be able to choose what to eat, where to roam, and with what other animal to mate. Whether this is instinct or some form of limited choice is for theologians, philosophers, and environmental scientists to debate. In the highest form of life on earth, that of human beings, there is the ability to reason and to choose. Thus human beings can make decisions about a variety of things: what to eat, where to live, with whom to mate or not to mate at all, how to live life, how to love or to hate.

In order to choose, one must have options. Thus, finding and evaluating options is a necessary step in the decision-making process. An option is available to me only if I see it and accept it as possible. For example, I decide to lose twenty-five pounds. But if I do not believe that I have the willpower to exercise and diet, then it cannot and will not happen for me. Losing twenty-five pounds is not a viable option. It is wishful thinking.

In making decisions as a couple, it is necessary to find options that are viable for both parties. The qualities of intimacy (chapter 2) and the attitudes that foster intimacy (chapter 3) are helpful in uncovering options that are acceptable to both spouses. If we are open to each other, I will keep an open mind to my spouse's preferences rather than concentrate only on my own. If we trust each other, I will not fear my spouse's suggestions and will come to accept them more readily. If we live life as mystery we can let go of control and trust God with options that may be too much of a stretch for us. If I remember that I am not happy unless my spouse is happy, I can seek alternatives that are good for both of us rather than those that are good only for me.

Fears and obstacles to intimacy can limit our options. If I fear losing my spouse's love, I will opt for some guarantee of that love. If I am afraid that I am failing to fulfill my responsibilities at my place of employment, I will probably spend more time working and will then have less time to spend with my spouse. If I fear being unlovable, I will choose the options that satisfy my need for love. Qualities that foster intimacy increase mutually viable options. Fears and obstacles to intimacy limit mutually viable options.

When we make decisions as a couple, each spouse still makes his or her individual decision. When our individual choices are the same, we have a mutual decision. My choice becomes our choice when both of us choose the same thing. We may differ on the reasons for the choice or the methods of choosing, but as long as we choose the same thing we have a mutual decision, one that both of us can accept. Thus, we enter into the covenant of marriage when both of us come to desire and accept marriage. It does not matter why or how we decide to choose marriage. It is only important that we both choose marriage.

Most often joint decisions are individual decisions that agree. But joint decisions can also be made by one spouse allowing the other to make the decision for both of them. A good example is in the movie *Casablanca*. Rick (Humphrey Bogart) and Elsa (Ingrid Bergman) are madly in love with each other. They met in Paris and fell in love. They were then separated for a few years and by chance met again in Casablanca during World War II. In the time of separation, Elsa, not knowing whether Rick was dead or alive, married another man. She had to decide whether to stay with her husband or go with Rick. In one moving scene, Elsa asks Rick to decide for both of them. Rick, the counter culture hero, decides to let Elsa go so she can help her husband fight the Nazis. In real life, generally the circumstances surrounding these kinds of decisions are not this dramatic. But if we can truly give our spouse the freedom to make the decision, good joint decisions can be made. In our family of four, choosing a restaurant that all of us like is often difficult. It works for us when we take turns in choosing the restaurant.

Qualities and attitudes that are conducive to intimacy will be helpful in the decision-making process. Fears and obstacles that hinder intimacy will limit options and compromise mutuality of choice.

B. Awareness of decision-making styles

Although it is not required for mutual decisions, understanding and appreciating my spouse's reasons and methods in making particular choices are helpful in making joint decisions. There are a number of self-reporting instruments available today that can help us understand our preferred manner of making decisions, of taking in and evaluating information, and of organizing and living our life. We recommend the Myers-Briggs Type Indicator (psychological) to all couples. (See Resources on page 141 for more information.)

The Myers-Briggs Type Indicator uses four preference scales to indicate a model of personality. The *extroversion—introversion scale* measures the preferred orientation of our energy. People who are extroverts get their energy from the outer world of people and activity. Introverts get their energy from their inner world of ideas and experiences. The *sensing—intuition scale* relates to how we take in information. People who prefer sensing acquire information that is real and tangible—what is actually happening. People who use their intuition acquire information by seeing the big picture, focusing on the relationships and connections between the facts.

The *thinking—feeling scale* indicates preferred style of decision making. People who prefer thinking look at the logical consequences of a choice or action. Those who prefer feeling consider what is important to them and to others involved. The *judging—perceiving scale* weighs how we organize our life. Those who prefer judging wish to live a planned, orderly life. They want to make decisions, come to closure, and move on. People who prefer perceiving want to live a flexible, spontaneous life. They want to go with the flow and keep their options open until the last minute.

Understanding our psychological type is helpful in relationships. When we understand that we prefer to draw our energy, to acquire information, to make decisions, and to order our lives in different ways, we can better accommodate these differences. Instead of allowing our differences to cause conflict and hinder communication, we can use these differences to reduce conflict and improve communication. We can understand that our spouse is not trying to make life difficult. It is just the way he or she prefers to act.

This personal example is illustrative of the usefulness of understanding our own and our spouse's preferences. Being extroverted, Bridget prefers to think out loud and to say what she is thinking in almost a stream of consciousness manner. I am an introvert who prefers to ponder a situation quietly and speak only after I have come to a conclusion.

One day out of the blue Bridget announced that she would like new kitchen cabinets. Forgetting that she is an extrovert, I was initially somewhat annoyed that she was planning to redo the kitchen without first discussing such a major project with me. I began to measure the kitchen cabinets in order to estimate the cost. I was hoping to show Bridget that replacing the present cabinets which, in my mind, were still functional and attractive, would be too expensive. But Bridget asked me why I was measuring the cabinets. "Because you want new cabinets," I responded. "No," she said. "I am only thinking about new cabinets and I have not decided that I want them." I should not have been annoyed. Bridget would have consulted me if she had decided on the cabinets. By the way, some years after this conversation, we did redo the kitchen and put in new cabinets.

C. Choices for life together

In life we must continually make choices. We can make new choices and we can affirm or change old ones. Before we were married, we made individual choices. After marriage, we make choices as a couple.

Marriage closes for us some options but opens up many choices for life together. We must decide

- how to relate to each other
- how to relate to our immediate and extended families
- whether and how many children to have
- how to relate to our friends
- whether and how to pursue our careers
- our preferred lifestyle
- how to use our time, talent, and money.

D. Shared value system

As adults, we base our choices on a value system that we have built up through our experience. I know and choose the higher good over the lesser good. However, sometimes a difficulty arises when we attempt to make decisions together. My value system may be different from that of my spouse. If our value systems are in conflict, then which one do we use? We can come to a mutually agreeable choice easier if we have a common value system that we both can accept. Bridget and I agree on the value system shown in the following diagram.

Our highest value is intimacy between Bridget and me and with God. This is followed by the value we hold for the people in our lives: our children, families, friends, and acquaintances. Next in this hierarchy of values are our careers and our work together. And finally, our talent, time, financial resources, and lifestyle are all valuable, but are less important to us.

In life, we desire and hope to have all of the above values. But the circumstances of life often dictate that we cannot have them all at the same time. Thus, we have to choose among good things. A common value system is useful because we can agree on the hierarchy of values. After we had our first child, most important to us was intimacy with each other and God, followed by the care of our child. Only then did we consider the lesser values of career and money. Bridget resigned her teaching job so she could spend time and energy with me and with Francis. It is human nature that we can make heroic sacrifices if we agree upon the reason for the sacrifices. If we do not agree, we will probably not make the sacrifices. Bridget would not have continued to teach just so I could have the money to buy my dream car.

Value systems change with our life circumstances. We were older when we married and our careers were already established. Therefore, having children was a higher value than our individual careers. But for younger newlyweds just getting established, their careers may have higher value than having children. In this case, they can choose to concentrate on their careers (a higher value) and postpone having children (a lesser value) for a few years.

A common value system may take some time and effort to develop. We begin by talking about our individual values and looking for common ground. In areas where there is conflict, we must be open to each other and reexamine our own values. Ultimately, I must be willing to change and make my hierarchy of values acceptable to my spouse. My spouse must do the same. When we mutually understand and appreciate each other's values, we can more readily find mutually acceptable options.

E. Perspectives on money, time, and sex

Managing money, time, and sex is a continuous task requiring decisions as a couple. This segment presents two perspectives on managing money, time, and sex.

Michael Lawler has published a survey that says most young couples find they do not have enough money, time, and sex.[1] These results are probably true for older married couples as well.

We are conditioned by our society to believe that we do not have enough money, time, or sex. Wayne Muller, in his book *Sabbath*, makes the case forcefully. He says,

> *Progress* is the road to the new and improved promised land. At the end of progress, we will all have peak efficiency, superior productivity, and an elevated standard of living. We will have thoroughly mastered nature and all its inherent problems, we will all live in a place and time in which all will be well, all disease cured, and all wars ended, with a chicken in every pot. . . .
>
> What we are building for the future is infinitely more important than whatever we have right now . . . our riches exist always to be mined and harvested in the future. . . .
>
> If the promised land is the good and perfect place, then where we are now must be an imperfect place. . . . If the future is sacred, then the present is profane. . . . Today—because it is not yet perfect—is always a bad day.
>
> This means that we have to work hard and long and never, ever rest because our main task is to get the hell out of here.[2]

It is when we experience over and over again that progress is unsatisfying and unfulfilling that we begin to question our assumptions about progress. It is out of frustration that we go back to examining our vision and our essential values. We begin to ask the question of how money, time, and sex relate to our vision and essential values.

If our deepest desire is for love and intimacy, how much money do we really need? Money of itself, no matter how

---

[1] Michael G.T. Lawler, *Time, Sex, and Money: the First Five Years of Marriage* (Omaha: Center for Marriage and Family, 2000).

[2] Wayne Muller, *Sabbath: Finding Rest, Renewal, and Delight in Our Busy Lives* (New York: Bantam Books, 2000) 77–78.

much we have, will not guarantee a successful relationship. In fact, the pursuit of money is often detrimental to
achieving intimacy. The answer may be that we do not
need more money, but need to be satisfied with what we
have and use it to foster our relationship. When we take
the perspective that we have enough money, we open up
options that do not require money. We see how we can
achieve our objectives of love and intimacy without the
need of money. We simply trust that God will provide for
our needs.

> Jesus said to us disciples, "Therefore I tell you, do not
> worry about your life and what you will eat, or about your
> body and what you will wear. For life is more than food
> and the body more than clothing. Notice the ravens: they
> do not sow or reap; they have neither storehouse nor barn,
> yet God feeds them. How much more important are you
> than birds!" (Luke 12:22-24)

And what about time? We hope and live for those times
when we can be alone and intimate without distractions—
time to rest, pray, contemplate, recharge our energies, and
time for retirement.

These times that we anticipate are certainly needed. But
if our fixation is only on these enjoyable times, then we
lose the value of the here and now—the time we spend on
raising our children, developing our careers, caring for our
loved ones, maintaining our household. The necessary
chores prevent us from the time we want. So we have to
find ways to do fewer of the necessary things in order to do
more of the desired ones. We have to make progress.

How much lived-for time do we really need? How much
is enough? If we believe our primary goal is intimacy, then
it is important that we use the precious time we have to
grow in love and intimacy.

Very early in my professional career, I, Jerry, heard good
advice from a motivational speaker who suggested that we

make a list of everything we do. The list was to have three headings: things I must do, things I want to do, and things I neither must nor want to do. His advice was to tear up the third list and never do those things again.

Even better advice is to move things on the "must do" list to the "want to do" list. Each morning I enjoy reading the newspaper, but I am also responsible for washing the breakfast dishes. In the past there was a conflict because I did not have time to do both. Recently I adopted a new attitude. I may choose to enjoy reading the paper and not do the dishes (until later!) without feeling guilty. Or I choose to do the dishes and not feel that I have sacrificed reading the paper. Before making this decision the conflict did not allow me to enjoy either the paper or the dishes. My new attitude gives me the enjoyment of what I choose to do.

We can also view our lovemaking from the perspective of what is essential to our relationship. Certainly lovemaking is essential to intimacy. In making love, we give ourselves to each other totally. But how often is enough? The answer may not be in how often but in how satisfying. Instead of trying to make love more often, we may want to find ways to make lovemaking more satisfying when we have the opportunity.

In summary, we can recognize two contrasting views of our resources of money, time, and sexual intimacy. One view is that we do not have enough and must work to get more. The other is that these resources are gifts from God and we have more than enough if we use them wisely to achieve the goal of growing in love and intimacy. The second perspective focuses on the essential—the hopes and dreams of our relationship. Time, money, and sexual intimacy are useful and valuable only if they are used to achieve our hopes and dreams.

Julian of Norwich (1342–ca.1416), the medieval religious mystic, is known for saying ". . . all shall be well, and all shall be well, and all manner of thing shall be well."[3] Whether all is or shall be well depends on how one defines "well." If well is the vision of love and intimacy, then all is well. God has guaranteed our success and provided all that we need. If well means we need more money, more time, and more sex, then all is not well, because we will never have enough.

F. Managing money

Earning and managing money is a difficult task, even for just oneself. Managing money as a couple has the added difficulties of making and honoring joint decisions. Conflicts arising from money issues have been identified as a major cause of divorce.

Conflicts

Making decisions as a couple can cause conflicts. We may not understand or appreciate our spouse's choices or needs with regard to money. Our value systems also extend to what money can buy. We may disagree on the worth of a particular item. For example, when we travel, I think motels such as Motel 6, Super 8, or Red Roof Inns are economical places to stay. They are generally clean, comfortable, and they provide a free continental breakfast. Bridget finds that they have thin walls, are noisy, have doors that open outside. She prefers a Sheraton, Marriott, or Hilton. I am reluctant to pay double or triple rates just for the small amenities like shampoo and lotion in the bathroom. So now we compromise; we stay at a Fairfield Inn or a Hampton Inn.

I also have a great love for Celtic music. It is inspirational for me when I am feeling low, but also when I am in a good mood. I buy a lot of Celtic CDs. Bridget sometimes

---

[3] Julian of Norwich, *Revelations of Divine Love*, 13th Revelation, ch. XXVII, par. 56.

wants to know how much inspiration I need. Now, when preparing our budget, we discuss how each of us would like to spend our money and this is helpful.

Conflicts may occur because of different future expectations. Saving money for future hopes and dreams is a necessary part of a budget. We save for the dream home, for the education of our children, and for our retirement years. But how much we need to save will differ on what we expect of the future. Most of our savings are in the stock market. I expect at least a six percent annual gain since historically the stock market has averaged a ten percent annual gain. Bridget points out the recent four-year market recession (1999–2003) and that we cannot count on a six percent return on our investments. I believe we have saved enough for retirement, but Bridget does not.

We can attach false value to our hard-earned money. Some may use their annual earnings as a measure of self worth. Others may see money as a means to power and status. Desire for worldly goods drives others to accumulate money. All these desires will hinder our ability to use money to achieve our goal of love and intimacy, and cause conflicts in our management of money.

Money can be used to control and manipulate. It sometimes becomes the principal factor in the power struggle between spouses. Whoever controls the money generally also controls other aspects of the relationship. Wives who do not work outside the home may feel especially vulnerable if their husbands earn and are in charge of all the money.

Trust is also an issue. Can I trust my spouse to manage my hard-earned money? Do I need to express my opinion on every purchase decision, even the minor ones? Once we have prepared a budget, can I trust my spouse to live within the budget and honor the agreement? Conflicts can arise from the lack of trust.

Yet, despite the difficulties and the conflicts, managing money together can be a positive, even a joyful aspect of a good marriage. It is something we do as a couple and we should enjoy it. If we focus on the essentials and use money to finance the objectives of our relationship, our budget becomes an action plan to achieve our hopes and dreams. Preparing the budget becomes an expression of our desire for intimacy, an affirmation of our mutual goals, and a renewal of our fidelity and trust in the covenant.

Again, and as with all aspects of a good relationship, the qualities and attitudes that foster intimacy will be helpful in preparing and then living within the budget. Trust, openness, fidelity, and self-sacrifice are especially needed. Fears and tendencies that hinder intimacy will also hinder making good budget decisions.

Preparing a budget

Since a budget is an action plan to implement our hopes and dreams, a good way to start the process is to share those hopes and dreams. We must first determine the essential goals of our relationship. The goals and the right attitude will guide us to the right questions in developing an action plan.

If we want money for a vacation so that we can spend time together away from the children, then we might ask ourselves, "Where can we get more money?" The answer may be in working harder and longer, which results in less time together. Or we could try the lottery or other get-rich-quick schemes, which generally are not successful.

If we focus on just the desire for more time together, we could ask, "How can we, in our present circumstances, find more time to be together?" The answer will be different from how we can acquire more money. It may be that we work less and spend less. We can send the kids to Grandma for a few hours and spend that time picnicking in the park. If we focus on the essential, we will find more viable options.

A budget is a spending plan to pay for all necessary and desired objectives with available resources. A balanced budget has available resources equal to the overall spending. A budget, therefore, must include all anticipated expenses as well as expected income. We will not guide the reader on how to prepare a joint budget. There are many available resources to help those who are new to the process. We recommend a simple budget book or the computer program *Quicken*.[4]

We do want to offer a few suggestions. For those who are planning marriage, one simple way of starting to prepare a joint budget is to put your individual budgets together. The combined budget is a record of your income and expenses as a couple. Even if the new combined budget is balanced, you will need to look for ways to save money because you will have new items in the budget, i.e., a new home, college education for children, retirement, etc. You can save by cutting items you do not necessarily want or need. All of us can find ways to save money: we can avoid frivolous spending and giving in to high-powered sales pitches, or we can sacrifice a few of the luxuries we enjoyed as single persons. If we need to make hard choices and give up something we really want, we must look at our value system. What is most important to us and what is there that we might give up?

Most "how to" books on budget preparation will give sample budgets that consist of lists of ordinary expenses such as house payments, food, clothing, health insurance, transportation, and incidentals. Some budgets are very detailed with many subcategories and spending plans by month or week. These sample budgets are for people with Myers-Briggs *Judging* preference. All the spending options and the level of spending are set before the start of the fiscal year. This kind of budget will be very difficult for the Myers-Briggs *Perceivers*, who want to be flexible and keep

[4] Intuit, *Quicken* (Miami, 2003).

their options open until the last minute. The Perceivers do not know how much money to set aside for a vacation since they do not know until the last minute whether they want to go on a vacation. Perceivers do have budgets but they build flexibility into them. They might save money for several purposes: go to the theater, take a vacation, and/or dine out at a fancy restaurant. They can then be flexible. If they spend the money on the theater, they may have to forego the vacation. Perceivers need to check often to see that their funds are not depleted before the end of the year. Persons with the Myers-Briggs Judging preference will be checking constantly. If the January heating bill is over the budget, they will adjust by turning down the thermostat in February so that they will have a balanced budget at the end of the year. The bottom line is that a budget must be prepared that is acceptable to both parties.

Having a joint budget is generally easier to manage than two individual budgets. But there are reasons for separate budgets and checkbooks. When we were first married, Bridget had a fear of losing her independence and of being free to make her own financial decisions. She wanted to keep her own checkbook. That worked out well and after our first year of marriage she gained enough trust in me to let me manage the money. We then merged the checkbooks.

Borrowing money is not always bad. It all depends on the purpose of the loan. If we borrow to achieve an objective that we cannot achieve without borrowing, such as paying for the children's or our own education or buying a house, then securing a loan is good. It is a means to a desired objective. But if we pay a high interest rate on a loan and then spend the money on an excessive lifestyle, the borrowed money has been squandered, and we put a burden on our future without any present benefit.

Living within the budget

A budget is only successful if both spouses live within it. I will stay within the spending guidelines only if I wholeheartedly agree with them. If I do not agree, I can grudgingly curtail my spending to stay within the guidelines and will probably build up resentment while doing it. Or I can refuse to spend within the budget and break the trust of my spouse. Budgets are contractual agreements between spouses, and they can always be renegotiated. It is better to renegotiate than to break the trust of one's spouse. Keeping a record of income and expenses is important to track how we are doing with respect to the budget plan. A budget book or *Quicken* is helpful here. Not knowing where the money is going or who is spending the money can lead to conflicts.

As circumstances change, budgets need to be adjusted. Even when preparing a budget some flexibility is desirable.

Suggestions

Professional advice is helpful in managing money. There are many free sources on the Internet for securing help in preparing budgets and managing money. I, Jerry, find that the free help is often as good as the advice one pays dearly for when consulting a professional. To get good advice, I need to ask the right questions and find the right source. In order to do this I need to be clear about my objectives. If I inquire about making a quick million, an advisor may suggest the lottery, risky investments, or some other "get rich quick" schemes. If I want to know how to save for my child's college education, the advisor may recommend investments that offer good returns and moderate safety. If I do not know my objective, I will ask the wrong questions and probably get the wrong advice. I need an advisor who can understand and appreciate my goals and who can advise me on a plan to achieve them. I should stay away from someone who is just trying to sell his product, especially if the product does not fit my objectives.

There is also professional help for those in deep financial trouble. Advisors will help negotiate with creditors and prepare a plan to reduce or eliminate the debt.

We can buy life insurance, disability insurance, health insurance, and long-term care insurance. But none of this insurance will necessarily provide us with financial security against unemployment. Federal unemployment insurance is insufficient for long-term unemployment. Rather, our financial security lies in our ability and willingness to earn money. Two examples illustrate this statement. We have a friend who lost a high-paying job. He was so devastated that for a long time he would not accept another position that paid less than the one he lost. Thus, he took himself out of the job market and created an even more serious problem for himself. In contrast, when my uncle came to the United States, he could not work as a certified public accountant because his degree was not recognized in this country. But he found employment, first as a cab driver and then as a restaurant manager until he became a licensed CPA in the U.S.A.

G. Managing time

Many people in our American society feel they are too busy. They do not have enough time to do what they must do and what they want to do. They feel irritated when they can do little to relieve their busyness. Yet, if we focus on the essentials of our relationship, we see there is much we can do to control our busyness. First, we can change our attitude. If we worry about having too much to do, we add anxiety and frustration to our busyness. We reduce our effectiveness, for anxiety and frustration drain our energy.

I, Jerry, get anxious about things that I prefer not to do but know I must do. I procrastinate and try to put off doing those things. But that just increases my anxiety because I still must face doing the unpleasant things. I begin to feel tired and drained. I can help myself by performing the unpleasant tasks right away so that the anxiety will not drain my energy.

If we do the necessary things and not worry about how much we can finish, we can reduce our anxiety and frustration. We can then focus our energies on the tasks at hand and be more effective in doing them.

We can also examine what we believe we really must do and what we want to do. Sometimes we put on our "must do" list things that are not really necessary. A frustrated wife once asked her friend how she managed to be a good mother and wife, have a full-time job, and keep the house in good order all at the same time. Her friend's brief answer was simply, "Lower your standards." Again, focusing on the essentials will allow us to find out what is necessary and what is not. All of us can shorten our "must do" list.

There are times when a friend, a boss, or even a family member asks us to do things that we really feel we do not have time to do. But to refuse will cause us to feel guilty. If agreeing to do the chore puts a burden on us, then we sometimes do ourselves a disservice by doing it. We are depriving ourselves. I find it easier to say no to someone than does Bridget, who is a high Myers-Briggs *Feeler*. We can reduce our busyness by saying no more often. But even if we say yes, we will reduce anger and save energy if we can accept the yes as something we want to do and not as something forced upon us.

I find that my energy level increases when I do the things I like to do. I do not worry about not having enough time. I can work late into the night and sacrifice sleep when I am doing something I enjoy. I feel frustrated when I have to do chores I do not enjoy before I can get to do what I want to do. Now I try to put aside the other things and do the enjoyable things as much as possible. Also, I try to move things in the "must do" list to the "want-to-do" list.

Rest is also helpful to relieve stress and to regenerate energy. Most of us wait until we have completed all our tasks before we rest. And it follows that if we do not have enough time to complete our tasks, we never have time to rest. We need rest if we are to be energized and effective in our work. During even a short rest period, we can reorganize our priorities, regain our balance and our enthusiasm, boost our confidence, and renew our commitment to our essential goals.

H. Exercises and reflections

Reflect on each of the following questions and share your answers with your spouse and with the group.

1. Making decisions as a couple
Choose a significant decision that we have made recently.

- How did we come to agree on the decision?
- What were my reasons for the decision?
- Were my reasons for the decision the same or different from that of my spouse?
- Was the decision satisfactory for both of us?
- Was the process satisfactory for both of us?

2. Hierarchy of values
- Rank the following in terms of value to myself: my relationship with (a) my God, (b) my spouse, (c) my children, (d) my family, (e) my spouse's family, (f) my friends, (g) my spouse's friends, (h) my career, (i) my spouse's career, (j) my own interests, (k) my spouse's interests, (l) money, time, talent, and lifestyle.
- Compare my hierarchy of values with that of my spouse. Can we agree on a common value system?

- Explain to my spouse why and how I ranked the values as I did.
- Try to understand and appreciate my spouse's values.

3. Perspectives of money, time, and sexual intimacy

- Am I frustrated with the constant need for more money, more time, and more sexual intimacy?
- How can we use our money, time, and sexual intimacy to fulfill our deepest desires?
- What are some concrete ways we can better use our available resources?

4. Managing money

- In money matters, on what issues have we experienced conflict?
- What are the causes of the conflict?
- Were the conflicts resolved?
- Do we have a budget? If so, did we prepare the budget together?
- Did we share with each other the essential goals of our relationship?
- Does the budget reflect these essential goals?
- Are we using our money and time to reach these essential goals?
- If we are not doing the above, would it make sense to do so in our next budget?
- Do I think having a common value system will make it easier to make budget choices?
- Did we have to make choices and sacrifices according to our hierarchy of values?
- Who is the principal money manager in our marriage?
- Are we both comfortable with that?
- Does the money manager communicate adequately with the non-money manager?

5. *Keeping the budget*

- Do I wholeheartedly agree with the budget we have now?
- Is the budget realistic?
- Can we keep our spending within our budget? If not, should we renegotiate or revise the budget?
- Do we keep track of our spending?
- How often do we check to see if we are spending according to the budget?
- Do we blame each other for going over the budget? How do we resolve these disputes?

6. *Managing time*

- Do I feel I am always too busy? If so, how do I relieve the stress of being too busy?
- Does it make sense to reexamine my perspective on having enough time?
- Does changing my perspective reduce anxiety, stress, and frustration?
- Does it make sense to reexamine my "must do" and "want to do" lists? Is there any way to shorten the lists so that I have less to do each day?
- Does it make sense to rest so that I can be more effective and productive? Do I make time to rest during my busy day?

6

Making Love in a Sexually Charged World

If God is Love, do we "make God" when we make Love?

A. New wine for new wineskins

In the area of sexuality, we are walking on the edge of the cliff of a traditional morality that overlooks a sea of contemporary amorality. On the cliff our churches preach commitment before sex. In the sea the untamed energy of the Eros is promoted 24/7 through our media, at the grocery store checkout lanes, at the quick trip fuel stations, and in the unsolicited Spam popping up on our home computers.

How can we possibly hear or find God amidst this blaring of sex? In Genesis we read, ". . . in the divine image God created them; male and female God created them" (1:27). The Creator was not speaking simply of sexual pleasure without commitment. In the creation story, Adam and Eve belonged to each other; they claimed each other; they were an expression of God's covenant love.

As we slowly and cautiously shift from a "me" generation to a "we" generation, we are being afforded the opportunity to discover anew the mystical, magical, and mysterious energy of sexuality in a marital union.

Shift from functional to relational understanding of marriage

A significant shift in understanding sexuality today is the movement from a functional to a relational concept of lovemaking. For centuries sexual intercourse in marriage was viewed only for its procreative function—heirs for the throne or workers for the fields, depending on the strata in which persons were born. In addition, sexual intercourse was patriarchal in mode. Women were the property of males; the father handed his daughter over to her husband as property. The fact that husbands had sexual intercourse with mistresses and other available women was accepted, but married women were not allowed to have intercourse outside of marriage and were punished severely if they did. In an effort to protect unmarried women, particularly peasant women, from being sexually exploited, the Church in the Middle Ages stepped in to regulate marriages and took from the civil government the power of declaring marriages valid.

Procreative and unitive dimensions of lovemaking

In the pre-Vatican II Catholic Church, the Code of Canon Law of 1917 states that the primary purpose of marriage is the procreation and nurturing of children; its secondary purpose is the remedying of concupiscence (inordinate desire). Not terribly romantic, is it?

The 1960s saw a paradigm shift that could not be ignored. In the Catholic Church, the Vatican II documents spoke of the purpose of marriage as being procreative *and* relational. "Authentic married love is caught up into divine love and is directed and enriched by the redemptive power of Christ and the salvific action of the Church . . . spouses are penetrated with the spirit of Christ."[1]

The women's movement, coupled with the availability of the pill, ushered in a new and uncharted experience of sexual activities. We are only now beginning to study and understand how the women's movement, the sexual revo-

[1] Austin Flannery, O.P., Vatican Council II: *Gaudium et Spes* (Northport, N.Y.: Costello, 1980) par. 47.

lution, the civil rights action, and the Second Vatican Council have impacted and shaped our world today, especially in the area of sexuality. The Humpty Dumpty of Sex (traditional morality) fell off the cliff of tradition, and we are still scrambling to put Humpty Dumpty together again. But today it is not all the king's men who are patching Humpty together; it is women and men. A new Humpty will not sit on the cliff of tradition but on the cliff of lived experience. The new sexuality of marriage will be shaped by women and men who know that lovemaking is not only about procreation, but also about relating to one another in a manner that cannot be captured in a technique, but rather by a mutual desire to communicate to one another all that we are. Lovemaking means we risk vulnerability and open ourselves in a way that is a mystery and which, if steadfast, will indeed lead to the mystical. Our union with our beloved is a reflection and revelation of the mystical union of our God with us and us with God.

Exclusive love is freedom, not oppression.

In this mysterious, mystical, and magical sharing of lives, there is a bondedness and exclusivity that speaks of freedom and not of oppression. In earlier eras, when marriage was intended to provide heirs and farmhands, and where the women's role was to submit to their husbands and do as they were told, women and men were both oppressed. In today's marriages of choice, our exclusive love for one another is not oppression but freedom. It is only in commitment that I can risk revealing my deepest self to my spouse. Marriage is not a ball and chain; it is a freely chosen commitment to walk together along the path of self awareness and self communication which occurs in lovemaking in order that two might become one and witness God's love to our world.

B. The mystery of lovemaking

How do we ever understand the mystery of lovemaking, the unlocking of the God within us? It is a continual discovery. First, we must recognize that to enter into lovemaking we are entering into sacred space; we are on holy ground. A reverence for lovemaking is essential because we are touching the holy in the other. We become aware that lovemaking is transcendent, that lovemaking spurs us on to that which is beyond us, that lovemaking is indeed ecstasy, pleasure that moves to joy, tenderness that heals, fidelity that grounds us in who we are.

Power of lovemaking

Wrapped in these qualities, I am empowered to claim myself, to walk with the confidence of being claimed, being chosen, being cherished. My beloved to me and I to my beloved. I leave my bedroom not repulsed or violated or bored but energized with the sharing of love from one to another.

Does the above come easily and automatically? No, but it can come naturally if we reflect on who we truly are and what we truly desire. The concept is valid. The difficulty is that we are too tired, too stressed, too preoccupied, and too nonrevealed to risk the mystery of lovemaking. Michael Lawler's research at Creighton University in 2000 tells us that the three major issues of newly married, and I would add most married couples, are that couples have "no time, no sex, and no money."[2]

We are a worn out people, worn out from what Ronald Rolheiser calls pathological busyness, distraction, and restlessness.[3] We cannot capture the magic, mystery, and mys-

---

[2] Michael Lawler, *Time, Sex, and Money: The First Five Years of Marriage* (Omaha: Center for Marriage and Family, 2000).

[3] Ronald Rolheiser, *The Holy Longing* (New York: Doubleday, 1999) 22.

ticism of lovemaking if the most erudite journal we read is *The National Inquirer,* if our intellectual diet is prurient sound bytes, and if the sensational is more alluring than the nonsensational. Because sex sells, we are confused about the intimate experience of lovemaking. But lovemaking is not for sale. Lovemaking belongs to the lovers. It is their story, their sacred garden of Love.

How-to books and techniques have their place in understanding lovemaking but they are never to be used to replace the interior reflection and dialogue that must happen within and between married lovers.

We Americans tend to be problem solvers; we want to solve our sexual problems rather than take the time to explore the mystery. We continue to regress to the "all about me" perspective of lovemaking rather than to a covenant-centered perspective.

We have become inundated with a celebrity sexual permissiveness that has diminished if not destroyed the concept of sexuality being monogamous and reverent. We must delete this from our screen.

If we are to grow into the depth and the power of sexual, committed love, we need to be in a vowed union. In a public celebration we proclaim to the community gathered with us, "We belong to each other forever." Our vows confirm our commitment and reconfirm the vows of all those present with us. We need the power of the community to support and sustain us and confirm us in our decision to commit forever in good times and in bad. Like attracts like. We gain much support from spending time with and sharing our lives with people who share our values, particularly in regard to sexuality.

Energy of lovemaking

Rolheiser, in *The Holy Longing,* states, "Our culture is too naïve about the power of energy. We see nothing wrong in exposing ourselves to it in all its rawness. We are right in one way, erotic energy is good, there is nothing wrong with Aphrodite and Eros having sex under a tree. What is problematic is that this is not an event meant to be watched. It is too raw. Love is meant to be made behind closed doors. . . .The wisdom in the taboo against exhibition is not, first and foremost, about morality and sin. It is about protecting people's souls from the kind of unhappiness that [comes from] . . . anything that is so raw as to overstimulate our energies."[4]

Sacredness of lovemaking

We presently live in a "tell all" talk show culture where nothing is unspoken; nothing remains upon which to reflect or cherish. Mystery is dismantled. A side effect of the "tell all" culture is that we do not know how to hold in our hearts that which is sacred and personal to my spouse and me. We have become overstimulated sexually through our movies and videos, songs and commercials, dress and reality TV.

This overstimulation of the sexual energy has created a sexually charged world that never sleeps and has no boundaries so that we have eight-year-old females being looked upon and clothed as sex objects. We have eroded our vocabulary so that there are innuendoes about daily conversations; innocence has been exploited. Such trivialization of sex and its uprooting from the sacred grounds of married commitment impede our ability to grow into a healthy and holy understanding of lovemaking. It is up to us who value and revere lovemaking to reclaim its beauty and sacredness. We do that primarily by living lives of sacred sexuality.

---

[4] Ibid., 29–30.

C. Lovemaking: An act of hope, thanksgiving, reconciliation, and affirmation

Jack Dominian, in writing about the meaning of sexual intercourse, describes seven individual characteristics of lovemaking that are very helpful when reflecting on this subject. His words capture the magic, the mystery, and the mystical and are in direct contrast to what we hear in our "tell all" culture.

Dominian tell us that sexual intercourse is a body language of love in which spouses are talking to each other with their bodies.

As such, it has the following possibilities:

- It is a means of thanksgiving. Couples can thank each other not only for the act they have just experienced but for their mutual presence. They can say with or without words, "Thank you for being here; I am grateful for your presence yesterday and the day before and all the time we have been together."
- It is a language of hope. Through intercourse a couple can reassure each other that they are wanted and appreciated and that they would like to stay together in the future.
- It is a means of reconciliation. Every couple knows that many quarrels and arguments are partially resolved or finally reconciled in an act of love.
- It is the most economic means by which the sexuality of each other is reinforced in a unique way. The couple acknowledge each other's masculinity and femininity through one of the most powerful means of reinforcing the sexual identity.
- Intercourse is a recurrent confirmation of the personhood of each other.
- It is the means through which sustaining, healing and growth are affirmed.
- It is the means through which permanence is reinforced and finds regularly one of its most powerful meanings.[5]

---

[5] Jack Dominian, *Dynamics of Marriage* (Mystic, Conn.: Twenty-Third Publications, 1993) 74–75.

D. Befriending our desires

Philip Sheldrake also gives us some reflections on love-making that capture the magic, the mystery, and the mystical:

- To give and to receive sexually has a sacramental quality as long as it truly aspires to be a gift of *self* and a joyful receiving of another person, rather than merely an exchange of bodily stimulation.

Spirit touches spirit

- It is an "outward sign of inward grace" of a deeper inner reality. Appropriate sexual body language is a sacrament of Real Presence—both the true and unashamed presence of one person to another and, within that and cementing that self-disclosure, the Real Presence of the indwelling God.

"This is my body—my life—given for you."

- "And they recognized him in the breaking of the bread." And we may recognize God, too, in the breaking open of bodies, the breaking open of self, for each other.

Sexual union is eucharistic . . .

- . . . a liturgy that may heal and restore loving partners to a spiritual centeredness. When we freely unite ourselves to another, we come to know ourselves at the same time as profoundly self-possessed, rather than invaded or stolen. Here, desire becomes more than a physical urge and is discovered to be that power within us that enables us to overcome our fears of absorption.
- Shared sexual joy, as a step toward God rather than as a substitute for it, is a genuine act of worship, a genuine prayer.[6]

---

[6] Philip Sheldrake, S.J., *Befriending Our Desires* (Notre Dame: Ave Maria Press, 1994) 78–81.

E. Practical comments

Since I am the practical half of this duo, I would like to close this chapter with some practical comments about lovemaking.

A significant number of authors writing on the topic of quality sex and lovemaking in marriage remind us that there are gender differences in our expectations of lovemaking as well as for the purpose of lovemaking. Very often these different expectations and different purposes create conflict and frustration between husband and wife.

Most women need attention and support in the larger picture of marriage in order to be excited and desirous of sexual intercourse. John Gottman, in his book *Why Marriages Succeed and Fail,* states, ". . . men who do more housework and child care have better sex lives and happier marriages than others."[7] Need I say more?

It is very easy to get bogged down with the house, career, children, in-laws, parish council—the list is infinite—and we find ourselves exhausted. The last thing we want to do is to make love. In fact, it is as if making love is just one more thing on the list. How do we deal with this? First, I am not sure we ever truly resolve the issue of too many things zapping our energy. It is a continual battle. However, one thing that has worked for Jerry and me for many years, since our children were in the primary grades, was to take a twenty-four hour getaway at a nearby bed and breakfast. We explored a variety of B & Bs within a few hours drive of our home. We would drop our children off at school, arrange to have a close friend or family member pick them up after school and keep them overnight. We returned the following day in time to chauffeur them home after school. They enjoyed a day away from us and we enjoyed a day alone together. This kind of arrangement could

[7] John Gottman, *Why Marriages Succeed or Fail* (New York: Simon and Schuster, 1994) 157.

also be worked out with another couple with children attending the same school. You keep their children one evening and they care for your children on another. The twenty-four hour getaway is one of the simplest and best ways to revive the drooping sexual spirit.

What women need to be aware of is that for many men, making love is how they experience growing in love. The act of lovemaking becomes an act of love. It becomes a way to reconcile if there is conflict. Women, on the other hand, need attention, affection, and connection before they can enjoy lovemaking. If there is a conflict they want the conflict resolved before they make love. As John Gottman verifies, for many women, help with the domestic chores is a much better aphrodisiac than any expensive perfume. So, men, toss out your *Victoria Secret* catalogue and get thee to the laundry if you truly want to woo your woman.

F. Exercises and reflections

Reflect on each of these questions and share your answers with your spouse.

1. *Think about the difference between a self-centered perspective and a covenant-centered perspective of lovemaking.*

   a. *Self-centered perspective on sexual intimacy:*

      I seek sex for my own pleasure and to satisfy my sexual urges.

      I am worried about my sexual performance.

      If I am good, I attract many partners.

      If the act is enjoyable, it is because my partner and I perform well.

      If the act is not enjoyable, there is something wrong with my partner or me.

      I choose and rate partners on how well the act is performed.

I am not concerned with fidelity and commitment. In fact, that limits my freedom to choose and change partners.

b. *Covenant-centered perspective on sexual intimacy:*

I choose to give my total self to my spouse.

I am not performing; I am being myself.

No matter what happens in the act, our covenant relationship will go on.

Pleasure is an added gift and not an essential.

Love and not sexual performance is a criterion for choice of mate.

Fidelity and commitment are crucial because they are the foundations necessary for intimacy.

- Which is more prevalent in today's society?
- Which will ultimately bring lasting joy and intimacy?

2. Obstacles to lovemaking

- What obstacles keep my spouse and me from growing more intimate in lovemaking?
- Am I willing to discuss this with my spouse and make an effort to grow and learn in this essential area of our married life?

3. Creative communication

- What are some ways that will help me communicate with my spouse about our sex life?
- Have we had a serious discussion if there is a problem regarding our sex life?
- Have I tried writing a letter to my spouse regarding lovemaking problems?

4. Understanding lovemaking

Talk about the reflections of Jack Dominian's and Philip Sheldrake's approaches to lovemaking.

- Does any of it resonate with our own lived experience?

- Is it too lofty for me?
- Do I really believe that we can recognize God in breaking open our hearts and bodies to one another?

7

Conflict and Communication

*If we are to grow in love and intimacy, we must be able
to resolve our conflicts and communicate our being.*

A. Embracing a positive perspective

Consider the following hypothetical situations. I am
driving along the highway when I see my spouse's car in
the ditch, engulfed in smoke, looking like it will explode
into a ball of fire any second. I see Bridget frantically trying to get out of the car. Will I immediately stop my car,
jump out, and risk my life to save my spouse?

In this hypothetical case I am able to help Bridget get
out of the burning car, but the car is totaled. One week
after this incident, a Best Buy truck pulls into our drive-
way. The driver is delivering a $10,000 home entertain-
ment center that Bridget bought the previous day. The big
problem here is that such an expenditure is not in our
budget. How do I react?

In the first incident I know that I will not hesitate to risk
my life to save Bridget. I immediately run to the burning
car to help Bridget escape this life-threatening scare. In the
second situation, I balk at Bridget's decision to buy this expensive furniture because I know it is not in our budget
and what's more, Bridget did not consult with me before
buying it.

Why the difference in my reaction to the two situations?
It is because my perspective is different in each situation.
In the first case, my beloved is in danger and I will risk my

life for her. In the second case, it was business as usual and Bridget violated our contract and my trust.

Fortunately, these are hypothetical cases. Bridget is safe and sound; the car is intact; and we do not own a $10,000 home entertainment center.

Our perspective on any situation is important because we act out of it. Our perspective contains our view of the situation, our interpretation of its meaning, our motivation for action, and our analysis of what action is needed.

Maintaining a positive perspective on our marriage is important for all aspects of the marriage, especially for conflict resolution and communication. When I am hurt by my spouse, when I am in conflict with my spouse, when I am disappointed by my spouse, I can take the perspective that my spouse does not love me anymore. Then I may want to get back at my spouse or even seek dissolution of the marriage. Or, I can take the opposite view that, even though we are in conflict, my spouse still loves me. I will then try to reestablish the relationship.

In the hypothetical cases, I can also take different perspectives. In the first case, I can conclude that Bridget was driving too fast, ran into the ditch, and totaled the car, so should I risk my life to save her? In the second case I may come to the conclusion that Bridget won the lottery and wanted to surprise me with a gift of fancy new furniture.

In all perspectives, we draw inferences on our intentions from our analyses of the situations. If, by some action, my spouse hurts me, I may conclude that my spouse does not love me anymore. Or I can believe that my spouse still loves me and that our conflict will be resolved. We really do not know our spouse's intentions. Both conclusions are leaps of judgment. But which judgment is correct? In a covenant marriage, the judgment that my spouse still loves me is correct for we pledge to be faithful to the covenant. We did not deny that there will be conflicts along the way.

B. Distinction between a difference of opinion and a conflict

Knowing the difference between conflicts and differences of opinion is helpful in recognizing conflicts. This difference may not be clear to those who have not experienced a major conflict. The following conversation between Bridget and me is an illustration of a difference of opinion that turned into a conflict. We were driving on I-55 from St. Louis to Chicago. I was behind the wheel. There was a car in the passing lane going the same speed as the car in front of me. I wanted to pass. I pulled into the passing lane, moved closer to the car in the passing lane, and flashed my lights. Here is our conversation.

Bridget: "You are getting too close. Don't tailgate."

Jerry: "I am not close. I am not tailgating. I am trying to get him to move over and let me pass."

Bridget: "You are tailgating. You are going to get us killed."

Jerry: "Who are you for? For me or this *#%* ahead of me?"

Bridget: "You are so stubborn, just like your father. You are going to get us killed. I don't want to ride with you anymore."

Jerry: "Now you are dragging my father into this. Who do you think you are? You think you are always right. Well, you are not!"

In this conflict mild irritation becomes anger, and feelings get hurt. The emotional mayhem was way out of proportion to the difference of opinion. I can discuss and even argue vehemently over a difference of opinion without becoming angry and hurt. But when the dispute becomes personal, when I become angry and experience hurt feelings, then the clash has become a conflict.

C. Conflicts will occur in relationships

Conflicts are a naturally occurring phenomenon in marriages. They occur in every marriage. Couples who claim that they do not have conflicts are either not being honest with themselves, or they are suppressing their feelings.

Conflicts occur for many different reasons. Most of all, they occur because it is difficult for two persons to grow to be one. Despite our best intentions, we will occasionally do or not do things that irritate, frustrate, and anger our spouse. When intentions are misread, hurt is added to the anger and frustration. Conflicts can arise from miscommunication, unawareness of my spouse's needs, unresolved personal issues, outside pressures, lack of trust, different moods, and many other reasons. Conflicts that recur and that seem impossible to be resolved may be caused by deep-seated fears.

It is popular belief that conflicts are responsible for the breakup of many marriages. However, if we can resolve the conflict by reestablishing the relationship, the marriage will be strengthened. If we do not resolve the conflict or do so in an unsatisfactory way, the marriage will suffer. Eventually, the marriage will dissolve.

D. In the heat of the argument

If we want the marriage to last we must resolve conflicts and reestablish broken or bruised relationships. The first step is to fight fairly during the heat of the argument. This means that we do not use behavior that will cause irreparable damage to our relationship. Remembering that we still love one another will help us control our behavior during the conflict. We must control our anger so as not to hurt our beloved. Certainly any kind of violence, be it physical, psychological, or verbal, is prohibited in a quarrel between lovers. Criticism, contempt, defensiveness, and withdrawal are to be avoided. Thus, even in the heat of battle we are thinking of reconciliation and preparing for the resolution of the conflict.

E. Resolving conflicts

Ways to resolve conflicts

There are several ways to resolve conflicts, but only one will heal our hurts and reestablish the relationship. Naturally, in the heat of the argument, I want the "I win; Bridget loses" end result. I want Bridget to admit that she is wrong, but Bridget says that will never happen so I am still waiting and sulking. I then hope that maybe a friend will tell Bridget she is wrong in holding her strong opinion in this particular situation. But that also does not happen and so there is a standoff. I know that if I can prove Bridget wrong, she will be upset and then we will both be unhappy and the conflict will continue to be unresolved. One of us must give in for harmony in the marriage to be restored.

Another way to resolve a conflict is to "build a wall around it" and declare the conflict off limits. Some couples use this method when the conflict is too heated and seems impossible to resolve. This method can, at least for a time, keep the couple civil to each other. But the wall prevents growth in intimacy. Love and intimacy cannot remain static. If we do not grow more intimate, we will drift apart.

In the classic 1939 film *Gone With The Wind*, based on the book by Margaret Mitchell, Clark Gable as Rhett Butler and Vivian Leigh as Scarlett O'Hara left many conflicts walled up and unresolved. In the end, Rhett said to Scarlett, "Frankly my dear, I don't give a damn." If there is anger, hurt, and even hate, there is something left in the relationship. But when we don't care anymore, then the relationship is dead.

Walling up a conflict is different than letting go of a potential conflict. In many cases we choose to let go of small hurts and irritations. People in a second marriage often speak of the need to "pick your fights." They do not want to confront each other on every hurt, slight, or irritation. They choose to let the minor squabbles pass and try to resolve the major conflicts. People who have grown intimate over time have built up a reserve of trust and forgiveness that allows them to let go of small hurts. Letting go is good for the relationship if they can truly forgive and forget.

Compromise is good and necessary for relationships. It is a good way to settle differences of opinion. But compromise is not a good way to settle conflicts. When emotions run high, I don't even know what constitutes a good compromise. What is a compromise for Bridget and me on tailgating? Agree to follow at only a certain distance? Consult an expert on tailgating? Do not travel together in the same car? But even if there is a compromise, our anger and hurts are not alleviated. We still keep score and look for ways to get back at each other. Yesterday Bridget kept her part of the bargain. Today Bridget didn't quite do her part, but I am a good guy and will let that go. However, if she fails tomorrow, I am going to be really angry.

Conflicts can be resolved in a manner that relieves the pain and anger that heals and strengthens the bruised relationship. Resolving conflicts in this manner requires a change in desire and perspective of both spouses. Our marriage covenant gives us the courage and generosity to make the necessary change of heart.

A conflict Bridget and I had illustrates a way to resolve conflicts with the perspective of covenant. This conflict arose in the thirteenth year of our marriage. We had just returned from Germany. I was there on business and Bridget accompanied me. I thought we had a good time although Bridget was on her own for a large part of our stay in Germany. One evening, looking definitely downhearted, Bridget came to me and said, "We have to talk." Now, I ask the guys reading this, "What is your normal reaction when your sweetheart approaches you and says 'we have to talk'?" Mine is panic. Bridget is upset and I am probably the cause. My first reaction is to plan my defense and my first line of defense is always, "I didn't do it." If that fails, my second line of defense is, "I won't do it again."

Bridget and I are not spontaneous, and we did not talk right away. We agreed to meet for a conversation in two hours. During that time I reflected and prayed. I realized for the first time in those thirteen years that Bridget still loves me and that we will still be in love after the conflict is resolved. With that realization, I had the courage to talk with Bridget without any planned defense.

In our talk, Bridget said she felt left out by me and by our sons. She felt that I cared only for myself and for what I wanted. She had complained to me about this many times before. I know that I am an introvert and a single-minded person. When I am focused on one thing, such as a sporting event with our boys, I can be unaware of Bridget or anyone else. Yet, in the past I could not accept or take seriously what Bridget said of me and I had a great fear of being abandoned by her. I thought she needed to see me as a warm and caring person or she would leave me. So I always protested to Bridget and accused her of misjudging me. I maintained that deep down I am a warm and caring person, even if I do not show it outwardly. But that night, because I had no defense, I really *heard* what Bridget was saying, and I realized that she knows who I am and still loves me. Because she loves me, she wanted to share her feelings with me. Because I trusted enough to let go of my fear and because Bridget risked vulnerability to share her feelings with me, we experienced the joy of reconciliation.

Self-centered and covenant-centered perspectives

Look at the contrast between the self-centered and covenant-centered perspective of resolving conflicts.

PERSPECTIVE I: SELF-CENTERED	PERSPECTIVE II: COVENANT-CENTERED
MY SPOUSE IS UPSET WITH ME	MY SPOUSE WANTS TO TALK TO ME
I HAVE A PROBLEM	SHE WANTS TO SHARE WITH ME
I MAY LOSE HER LOVE	I TRUST HER AND GOD'S LOVE FOR ME
I MUST PLAN MY DEFENSE	I AM OPEN TO HEAR HER
I DENY WHAT SHE SAYS	I HEAR AND ACCEPT WHAT SHE SAYS
I WILL COMPROMISE TO KEEP HER LOVE	I WILL FREELY CHANGE FOR THE BETTER
I WILL SEE WHAT I GET FOR MY SACRIFICE	LOVE, TRUST, AND INTIMACY GROW

The Cana Institute ©

Steps to conflict resolution

The covenant-centered perspective of resolving conflicts involves these logical, though not necessarily chronological, steps.

1. Call a time-out from the conflict.

Conflicts can not be resolved in the heat of the fight. Emotions are too high and reflection and change of heart are impossible. Therefore, a time-out to cool off and reflect is necessary. Take the time-out from the argument, but set a time to return to the conversation about the conflict. Otherwise, it will be more difficult to arrange a time for reconciliation.

2. Work off anger in a nondestructive way.

In the movie *Analyze This,* the gangster played by Robert De Niro is consulting a psychologist played by Billy Crystal.

At one point in the movie, Billy Crystal advises DeNiro to work off his anger. DeNiro takes out his gun, shoots a pillow six times, and says, "I feel better already."

3. Get over the denial.

When hurt, I like to go to my corner, brood, and feel sorry for myself. Why me? Why is Bridget dumping on me? It is not my fault. Bridget is wrong. Sometimes it feels good to brood. But I must get over it so I can get in touch with how I really feel and think about the conflict. I need to see the conflict objectively and realize what it is doing to our relationship.

4. I must change my perspective from what is in it for me to what is best for both of us.

Remember our love for each other. We still love each other and will remain in love after this conflict is resolved. Remember God's love and fidelity. Realize that the pain of separation far outweighs the pain of the bruised ego.

5. Ask God for the grace of trust, courage, generosity, and the desire to risk vulnerability.

6. Meet to share feelings, to say I'm sorry, to forgive, and to reconcile.

7. Dig down deep to find the causes of the conflict.

8. Freely make the resolution to change.

9. Experience the joys of reconciliation.

Resolving conflicts is not easy but the end result is ultimately joyful.

F. Communication is necessary for intimacy

The goal of intimacy is to be one with my spouse. To do so, I must reveal myself to my beloved and receive from my beloved her/his revelation. I reveal myself through communication. God is revealed to us through Jesus Christ, the prophets, and God's presence in our experience. I communicate myself to my spouse through our shared experiences.

G. Necessary steps for successful dialog

Communication is dialog, and for it to be true dialog each step in the process must be successful.

The dialog begins with the sender having a message to transmit to a receiver. The message sent can be only as clear as the message in the sender's mind. The message can be misunderstood or the wrong message can be sent if the message is not clear in the sender's mind.

The sender must risk vulnerability when sending the message or communication does not happen. In counseling married couples, Bridget finds that the fear of vulnerability prevents some couples from communicating with each other. The fear of vulnerability is especially great in sharing things close to our hearts. Many years of growing in trust are needed before we can share our deepest being.

The recipient must receive, understand, and accept the message. Messages sent when the recipient is distracted or not listening will not get through. That is why couples go off to be by themselves so that they can be totally focused and listen to each other. Each person must understand the message as well as the intention of the message. Once understood, the message must be accepted by the recipient. Because of my fear, it took me a long time to accept the message that Bridget was transmitting to me after our trip to Germany: that I am not a warm and caring person but yet she loves me in spite of these shortcomings. Accepting the message also risks vulnerability.

For a dialog to continue, the receiver must reply to the message. Again, the receiver risks vulnerability in replying. The dialog can break down at any of the above steps. Communication is not easy and is a skill every married couple needs to work on in their marriage.

H. Means of communication

How do we communicate? Most often we think of communication as verbal. Generally, we speak to each other. We can also write our message on paper or send it by e-mail on the computer. However, we communicate most often through all our shared experiences by "talking to each other" through our body language. Sometimes the message is confusing, especially if our body language says something different from our verbal language. By how we do things, we can communicate our energy level for and our enjoyment of the things that we do. Absence of communication is also a form of communication. Bridget is a high extrovert and very gregarious. When she is not talking, I know something is wrong.

I. What do we communicate?

If we are to be one, then we must reveal our total selves. What we communicate must be our total selves. Thus, all topics that reveal any aspects of us are the subjects of our communications. However, we most often communicate at only the surface level. We talk of our activities (What did you do at work today?), responsibilities (Who is going to pick up the kids?), our schedules (When will supper be ready?), the budget, the international, national, and local news, sports scores, television programs and movies, and the weather. This communication is good in that it keeps us connected and aligns our tasks and schedules. But our communication must go deeper if we are to reveal our total selves.

Less often, we communicate our needs, our complaints, and our requests for change. But seldom do we communicate our deep feelings, our moods, our hopes and dreams, our love and appreciation for each other. And yet, we must reveal our deepest being if we are to be one. So the goal of our communication is to trust enough and be free enough to communicate our inmost being. The key to successful communication is to build trust and to free each other from fear.

J. Suggestions to improve communication

There are many books on communication skills. This book is not one of them. However, we do want to offer a few suggestions:

- Maintain a positive perspective. This will be conducive to good communication. If we feel good about each other, we will find ways to communicate.
- Be aware of each other. If we are thinking of and feeling for each other, we are able to be aware of each other's moods and rhythms. We become attuned to each other. This will be conducive to good communication.
- Reflect on how you do or do not communicate now. Call to mind things you do that improve your communication and things that hinder it. Do more of the good things and eliminate the bad.
- Be inventive and proactive on how you communicate. If you cannot get the message across by one method, try another. In the movie *The African Queen*, Humphrey Bogart and Katherine Hepburn got each other's attention because they were marooned on a boat going down the Ulanga River in Africa.

K. Exercises and reflections

Take a few moments to reflect on the following and then share your reflections with your spouse.

1. On perspectives

- Recall an occasion that led you to conclude that your spouse does not love you anymore. What were the thoughts, feelings, and actions that resulted from this conclusion? How did you feel about these thoughts, feelings, and actions after the incident? Was your conclusion that your spouse does not love you correct?

- Recall another occasion that led you to conclude that your spouse does still love you. What were the thoughts, feelings, and actions that resulted from this conclusion? How did you feel about these thoughts, feelings, and actions after the incident? Was your conclusion that your spouse still loves you correct?

2. On conflict

- Reflect on a recent conflict in your marriage. What were your thoughts and feelings during the heat of the battle? Did you fight fair? Did your spouse fight fair? Did you take a time-out before resolving the conflict? Was the conflict resolved?
- If the conflict was resolved, how was it done? Was there a change of heart for both of you? Was resolving the conflict a joyful experience? What was the cause of the conflict?
- If the conflict was not resolved, can you now see ways to resolve the conflict? Will you try again to resolve the conflict?

3. On communication

- Reflect on how you communicate with your spouse.
- How often do you communicate verbally with each other? Do you write little notes and e-mails to your spouse? Are your written and verbal communications frequent enough?
- What do you communicate? Do you communicate deep personal feelings? Do you communicate your requirements, needs, and wants?

- What do you find difficult to communicate? How can you reduce the vulnerability in communication?
- Be inventive and creative. Come up with ways that can improve your communication.

4. Daily temperature reading

This is an exercise on communication put out by PAIRS, a relationship skill firm. (See Resources on page 141.) The exercise is intended for use on a regular basis. PAIRS recommends doing it every day. The exercise reduces the risk of noncommunication. Each spouse takes turns in sharing the following: (a) Appreciation; (b) New Information; (c) Puzzles; (d) Complaints and Requests for Change; and (e) Wishes, Hopes, and Dreams.

- Each person expresses some appreciation for the other. For example, I appreciate your good cooking. I appreciate that you pick up the kids when I get detained at work. I appreciate your sharing yourself with me last night. I appreciate your fidelity to me.
- New information. We can use this to keep each other informed. For example, I can tell my spouse that I plan to be away this weekend to attend a sporting event with our sons.
- Puzzles. We can ask whatever puzzles us about our spouse. It can even be a mild complaint posed as a puzzle.
- Complaints. Usually when we talk, complaints come at the top of the list and we never get past the complaints. In this schema they are fourth on the list, when spouses will more readily hear and accept them.
- Finally, we always end the conversation on a good note by sharing our hopes and dreams.

8

Mission:
Fruit of a Vibrant Marriage

A. Invitation to Mission

"I chose you and appointed you to go and bear fruit that will remain" (John 15:16).

Marriage reflects the union of Christ with the Church. In marriage we carry out Christ's mission to "love one another as I have loved you." It is our call, our mission as married couples to love each other, and from our love for one another, love will bear fruit.

We are first charged with the call to discipleship in baptism. Our wedding vows are an extension of our baptismal vows. The white garment of baptism that signifies we have been clothed in Christ is symbolically linked to the white wedding garment that many brides choose to wear on their wedding day as they enter into the mystery of living out the mission of Christ in company with their groom.

As couples discern the call to marriage, we need not check astrological signs to see if our signs are aligned. Instead, we need to consider whether our commitment to discipleship is aligned. In the exchange of marriage vows, in saying yes to one another, we are, in fact, saying yes to God—yes to all that God invites us to in our married journey as disciples of Christ. On this journey we will experience some good times, and some not-so-good times, and much of the journey will be very ordinary. As a couple, we say yes to all that is and to all that will be.

It is also important that we proclaim our marriage vows publicly and that we do so in the presence of our faith community. At baptism our family, friends, and faith community gathered round the baptismal font to welcome us and proclaim for and with us our choosing Christ. In marriage, we also gather our family, friends, and faith community, and joining with them we pronounce our vows of fidelity to one another and to God. We need the wisdom and the support of the faith community to witness to us, to mentor us, and to guide us toward becoming Christ to and for one another.

B. The marriage covenant is the foundation for mission

Rooted and grounded in our vowed love for one another, we reach out to the people in our lives with confidence and energy. Out of our own love springs a desire to love other people in our life. The marriage covenant is the foundation for all that we do beyond our marriage relationship. In the perfection of love we can love and serve our spouse and all others without limit. But in our imperfect world we must balance caring for our spouse with caring for others. We cannot tip the scale to one side or the other. God is in the both/and.

We cannot stay so focused on our marriage partnership that we become withdrawn or isolated from the larger society; nor can we become so extended that we stretch our covenant beyond its limits. Mission is the fruit of a healthy marriage, not an escape from an unhealthy one. It is only in healthy, adult marriage partnerships that this balance can be maintained.

C. Mission in our daily life

What does mission look like in the humdrum, day-to-day existence of married and family life? It looks pretty ordinary. For me, the ordinary world in which I am called to live a life of mission is in our home with my husband and children and in my work. I continually remind myself that my first and primary call is to my spouse. This is not always easy because I am an "out there among the people" kind of person, and I can very easily get so involved and engulfed in the world beyond Jerry that he does not always rank first. Indeed, he would say that frequently he feels he is only number nine or even ten on Bridget's list. This, of course, is a topic that necessitates conversation.

Being the extrovert, the "people person" of our duo, I sometimes tend to get immersed in the world beyond our partnership. Jerry, the introvert, non-people person, tends to withdraw from or even avoid people, especially those he does not know well. We are working to bridge this difference. I am getting better about not getting lost out among people, and Jerry is getting better about not going into his inner shell.

Part of the nitty-gritty service to others is balancing my primary commitment and my secondary commitments. For me personally and, I believe, for many others as well, it is a continual learning and discerning process.

D. Requirements for mission

We began with the vision and the ideal of marriage. What are the requirements for mission as a fruit of marriage?

The first requirement is exclusivity of our marital love. Choosing to be solely with one person in marriage is not limiting. It is freeing. Being loved exclusively by my spouse, I am free to be with and among others. I know who I am and to whom I belong, and others know that as well.

The second requirement is that our mission must be in some sense mutual. There needs to be some degree of appreciation and acceptance by my spouse for my mission in life and my commitment to others. For example, Jerry spends what seems like hours to me preparing his lectures for his classes at the university. While sometimes it feels like he has abandoned me for his ivory tower, there is a part of me that is very proud of his dedication and commitment to his students. We have a mutual commitment to share with others whatever talents God has given us. Jerry shares his talents with his students; I share my talents with my adult students and clients.

Because our commitment is mutual we can make requests of each other, and we call each other to accountability regarding balancing our time together and our time with others.

Aware of the exclusivity and mutuality undergirding our mission, we need to establish priorities and boundaries. Our marriage is our primary vocation and our first priority. If we have children, we learn to juggle the demands of parenting with the desire to spend quality time with each other; this is an ongoing challenge. Add to this the demands of family of origin, elderly parents, special-needs siblings, and the ideal and vision get blurry. It is so easy to become enmeshed in it all. Sometimes enmeshment is labeled mission, but it is not. Mission is rooted in spiritual freedom; it is not compulsive. We need always to call ourselves to our priority, to one another.

Establishing boundaries is essential. We maintain boundaries not to keep people out of our lives but to protect ourselves and our primary commitments. This is difficult for many of us, but good habits do form. If we learn to say no to what is not life-giving and what could pull us away from our primary vocation, we will discover that we are free to say yes to what we truly desire. We must remember that people who are needy do not respect our boundaries so we need to protect and respect our own boundaries. I have found that being married and having children grounds and anchors me for my ministry. My husband and children demand an authenticity from me that is freeing. They also love me for who I am and not for what I do for them.

Returning home from my duties at the Cana Institute refreshes and renews my spirit. I am loved for who I am—a wife and mother—more than for what I can do for another. Returning home also grounds my perspective of who I am and what is important in married and family life.

I have found that attending our boys' soccer games or track meets or even rugby games (rugby is still scary for me) draws forth from me a "mom piece" that is eventually recycled within me and shapes and forms my ministry to others. Learning to be with and for my spouse and children teaches me how to be with and for those with whom and to whom I minister. I believe that in a healthy marriage I am loved into being who I am by my spouse and I would never be who I am had we not met, fallen in love, and married. This "loved into being" occurs imperceptibly, droplet by droplet; and it is in the ordinary marriage and family time zone that it occurs.

Unnoticeably being loved into being, with an occasional neon lights event, is, in fact, the on-going conversion experience that each person is called to by baptismal initiation. We know that love is a choice, so each time we consciously choose to maintain our priorities and make healthy choices spiritually, physically, and emotionally, we are disposing ourselves to conversion. It is so simple that we miss it. As Americans, we have been formed in a lifestyle that says if it is not glitzy it does not count, it does not have value. As a result, the ongoing, ordinary, day-to-day conversion that marriage and family calls us to is tossed away, and we are subjected to the bare-all, tell-all competitive marathons presided over by the priest and priestess of the television talk shows, the effect of which is a distorted concept of marriage. Indeed, marriage is often perceived and depicted as boring. However, if we take note of how God is revealed in our world, often it is in the ordinary and boring. Consider the biblical stories of Abraham and Sarah, Moses tending the flock in his father-in-law's pasture, Mary in small town Nazareth, and Peter and his crew of Galilee fishermen. The call to mission is discovered and heard in the ordinary routine of life.

There is an ebb and flow of mission with my spouse and mission with others. It is a "both/and," and there is a rhythm to it that we need to recognize. Each person, each married couple has a rhythm and cycle as we mentioned in chapter 4. Mission is sometimes something very exciting and perhaps occasionally even exotic; but for most of us, mission is being open to the Spirit moving us within and without. At this particular time in our married life, Jerry's mission is to attend to his mother and her needs, both emotional and functional, as she adjusts to being widowed after sixty-four years of marriage.

Some years back, my mission was to attend to my mother in her elderly, widowed years as well as to be with siblings who were terminally ill. When our children were young, Jerry and I agreed that being with our children was a primary mission. We needed other elements of mission as well but, in terms of our value pyramid, our values were God, each other, and the children. Being open to the ebb and flow of our mission, recognizing shifts in our mission, and accepting that we sometimes move into desert moments in our mission, are all part of the formation experience to which we are called in marriage. Being open to God working in our lives is the foundation for a solid mission in marriage.

E. Transforming power of marital love

"I chose you and appointed you to go and bear fruit that will remain" (John 15:16).

Love by its nature bears fruit. Love must be expressed; it must go beyond itself. In healthy marriages we are called to be witnesses of God's love to and in our world. "See how they love one another." That is our mission, to be a revelation of God's love. Marriage is a billboard advertising God's presence in our world. We are the light that is not hiding under the bushel basket of narcissism and infatuation, but is glowing with love, the love of our spouse whose love mirrors God's love.

Married couples are called to mirror the Trinity in their married union. Love begetting love begetting love. Like the Triune God, we are one, yet distinct.

What makes us one is love, and the more in love we are, the more we become distinct, being loved into who we truly are.

Love begetting love begetting love. That the world may believe that it is God who has anointed us and sent us to:

> . . . bring good tidings to the lowly,
> to heal the brokenhearted,
> To proclaim liberty to the captives
> and release to the prisoners, . . .
> to comfort all who mourn, . . .
> To give them an oil of gladness in place of mourning,
> a glorious mantle instead of a listless spirit. (Isa 61:1-3)

F. Exercises and reflections

Take a few moments to reflect on the following and then share your reflections with your spouse and with your group.

1. On baptism and marriage

- Reflect on the connecting thread between my baptismal vows and my marriage vows.
- How do I experience my marriage vows being an extension of my baptismal vows?

2. On meaning of mission

- How do I understand mission?
- Am I ever tempted to substitute mission for my marriage?
- How do I manage to maintain boundaries and priorities between my marriage, my family, and my mission?

3. Marriage as foundation for mission

- Do I experience my marriage covenant as a foundation for my mission?
- Do I find strength and desire for mission springing from being intimate in my marriage?

4. Freedom for mission

- Has being rooted and grounded in my spouse's love provided me with an authenticity and freedom in mission?

5. My mission

- What is my primary mission now?
- To whom do I mission?
- Do I mission together with my spouse?
- If not, do I appreciate and accept my spouse's mission?

9

The Fruit of Love Is Joy

A. Our hopes, dreams, and vision

Thus far in this book we discussed choosing perspectives and behaviors that help us to grow in love and intimacy. The motivation to choose the right behaviors rests on our experience of joy, which is the fruit of love. We maintain that all of us have, sometime in our lives, been surprised by a joy that makes everything else seem inconsequential. We assume that all of us desire to grow in love and intimacy as a consequence of that experience. This little volume will be meaningless to those who have not experienced the joy of relationship. They will not understand nor accept that the deepest desire in our being is to love and be loved. We choose love and we choose life.

> I have set before you life and death . . . .
> Choose life, then, that you and your descendants may live,
> by loving the LORD, your God, heeding his voice,
> and holding fast to him. (Deut 30:19)

To choose life and love, we must prioritize our many desires and choose to love over all other desires. Without the experience of love, none of us can consistently choose love over all else.

We know that some of us cannot personally acknowledge any experience of love. Yet we believe that all of us, as adults, have had some taste of love and intimacy. Some of us may not realize it because of lack of reflection. For others, fear and past hurts may block our ability to accept love and joy. For these, we pray that the people in their lives and God will lead them to that experience of joy.

We who believe in the vision can imagine the fulfillment of that vision. What will heaven be for us?

All of us want heaven to be perfect. There will be no wars or conflicts; all people and nature will be perfect. Our minds and bodies will be perfect with no physical or mental limitations, no sickness or injuries.

Besides all of that, what would be the perfect relationship for us? My vision of the ideal relationship is that Bridget and I will be totally transparent to each other. There will be no misunderstandings and mistrust of intentions. We will spontaneously know, understand, accept, and cherish each other. There will be no rejection, betrayal, or loss. All fears and doubts will be replaced by total trust. We will find each other so beautiful and lovable that unconditional love is spontaneous. Our only desire will be to love and be united with each other. We will communicate that love constantly and unendingly.

These qualities of relationship also extend to all my loved ones who are in heaven with me. All in heaven will be in perfect relation of love and intimacy with each other and with the Creator, the Son, and the Holy Spirit. All of creation will be in perfect harmony.

> . . . as we are one, I in them and you in me,
> that they may be brought to perfection as one,
> that the world may know that you sent me,
> and that you loved them even as you loved me.
>   (John 17:22-23)

Thus, every moment of our eternal lives will be filled with joy and our joy will be complete.

> "I have told you this
> so that my joy might be in you
> and your joy might be complete." (John 15:11)

Live in the present

We look to the future and the perfection of relationship, not to live in anticipation of the future, but to help us live a better and more enjoyable present. Also, we look on our past experiences, not to live and hold onto the past, but to help us understand and appreciate the present. For we can live only in the present. The past is gone and can never be recaptured or recreated. The future is always beyond us. When we reach the future, it melts into the present.

Our vision and hope for the future will help us in our daily lives only if we truly desire and believe it can happen for us. If we truly desire intimacy, that desire can be the motivating force to live our lives in love and intimacy. If we truly trust God to grant us this gift of union, that trust can give us the courage to overcome fears and risk the vulnerability of relationship. If we believe the relationship is ultimately joyful, then we can live with our sorrows and loss with hope for the future.

But if our picture of heaven is just a pie in the sky dream and we do not believe that a perfect relationship is possible for us, then we will live lives of frustration and despair because we do not believe that we can ever attain what our hearts desire.

B. Fulfillment of hopes, dreams, vision

Our experience in what we are now doing leads us to believe and to trust in the vision. What are we doing, here and now as we grow in love and intimacy?

- We are sorting out our desires and continually and consistently choosing the desire to love over other selfish desires.
- With every act of love and intimacy, we are embracing more and more the qualities of intimacy.
- We are making the sacrifices to let go of fears, addictions, and obstacles to intimacy.

- We are building trust.
- We are faithful to each other and to the covenant.
- We are bearing sorrow and rejection without bitterness.
- We forgive and receive forgiveness.
- We reach out to those in our lives, caring for our loved ones as well as for strangers.
- We are missionaries of love to all those we touch.
- We act justly, honestly, and responsibly at work.
- We seek justice and peace in our homes, our country, the world.
- We are not defiled by shame.
- We experience the death and resurrection of the Paschal Mystery.
- We love and are loved.
- We have changed for the better.
- We are living holy lives.
- Our hopes, dreams, and vision are being fulfilled in our lives each day.
- Heaven is the consummation of what we are now living.

We do all of this in our plain and ordinary lives. We go to work, raise our children, attend to our family and friends, take time to relax and play, and we connect with others. These activities are certainly ordinary. But our intention to love and to be intimate makes these ordinary activities extraordinary. Because of our intentions these ordinary activities become the means to the fulfillment of our desire for love and intimacy.

Imagine what the world would be if everyone on earth believed and acted according to our hopes and dreams. Would this not be the perfect world that we hope for? If each of us would seek to grow in love and intimacy with those in our lives, would there not be a network of people in love that reaches everyone? And if all of us were in love, there would certainly be no wars, terrorism, injustice, oppression, and hatred. The world would be filled with peace, love, intimacy, mercy, and joy. With God's power, the consequence of what we do in our ordinary lives is the redemption of our world. Indeed, that is the only way the world can be redeemed, one person at a time. Each of us has to be redeemed personally before the whole world can be redeemed.

But, we observe, our daily lives are not like that. Often we fail to do what we should do. "The spirit is indeed willing, but the flesh is weak." At times we choose our selfish desires over the desire to love. We still face rejection and betrayal. We still find it difficult to risk vulnerability. Choosing love and intimacy is still very difficult. We continue to harbor deep fears and addictions and we cannot let go. Our distrust of each other and of God is still very strong. And we still do not know whether we can remain faithful to the covenant. Even though we keep trying, we fail more often than we succeed.

How, then, can or will we succeed? In time of self-doubt, we gain trust in God. As St. Paul realized, in his weakness he discovered God's strength.

In our mistrust of ourselves we discover that God trusts us. This is a consolation that I, Jerry, received while on retreat. My retreat director asked me to reflect on the question, "Does God trust me?" The answer in my prayer is, "God trusts me more than I trust myself."

We will succeed if we are faithful. Being faithful is to keep trying and never let failure be final. If we keep trying, God's power is sufficient. We see how God creates a huge tree from a tiny mustard seed. We see, in our own experience, how a tiny yes of "I will date you" blossoms into an everlasting love affair. With faith and faithfulness we cannot but succeed. Success is guaranteed.

C. Live on in faith, hope, and love

We trust our love for each other and God's love for each of us and that is enough. We still face all the dangers and uncertainties of this world. Our problems in life are not in anyway diminished. We still face sickness, war and terrorism, a lack of time and resources to do the things we want to do. We still face rejection, betrayal, and loss. We still face our own fears and addictions. We still worry about our loved ones. Yet, our love for each other and God's love are enough. Love is enough because we know it satisfies our deepest desires and makes all our cares inconsequential in comparison.

D. My prayer for you

Not all things have gone our way and not all our hopes have come true. Yet it is in reflecting on our experiences that our faith is grounded.

I have received so much love and consolation from Bridget. She has in so many ways expressed her love for me. I especially realize that she has to die to herself to love me.

My children have grown to be young men of faith. They have grown to become beautiful people, much more than I can ever plan or hope for. I know for sure that if I had controlled them they would not be the beautiful persons they are today. I enjoy them so much.

My family and my other loved ones, too, have also experienced the joy of God's love. In the face of all this, how can I not believe?

I know that we will face future trials, failures, and doubts. I know that Bridget still has some misgivings about me. But I trust that after she reflects on those doubts she will come to trust me. I appreciate that kind of trust more than blind trust given automatically and unthinkingly. I, too, have doubts about Bridget and about my ability to remain faithful to the covenant, but I believe that with God's grace, I will also come to greater trust.

Bridget and I have changed and grown in intimacy. We are more deeply in love and more intimate today than when we were first married.

Now my prayer each day is "Thy kingdom come." For, when God's kingdom comes, my fondest desire will be fulfilled: that all those I love will come to experience God's love for them and their joy will be complete.

I pray this for all of you who have read this book since you have become my friends through our common purpose and experience.

I pray that you set aside any worries about your marriage. Do not worry whether you will stay faithful to the covenant. Trust each other and trust in God. If you trust, a good, strong, and beautiful marriage is guaranteed.

Do not be disheartened about how difficult it is to die to self and to grow in intimacy. Instead, look toward the greatness of the call.

> I pray that each of us will day by day
> complain less and compliment more,
> expect less and enjoy more,
> worry less and trust more;
> then truly we will be blessings for many.

Resources

The following resources are available for those seeking help to strengthen their marriage.

- PAIRS (Practical Application of Intimate Relationship Skills) Information about PAIRS can be obtained on the Internet at www.pairs.com or by writing directly to Lori Gordon, PAIRS International, Inc., 1056 Creekwood Dr., Weston, FL 33326. Telephone 888-724-7748.

- Consulting Psychologists Press, Inc., 3803 East Bayshore Road, Palo Alto, CA 94303. Telephone 800-624-1765. Internet www.mbti.com. They can give you self-scoring Myers Briggs inventory forms and professional interpretation.

- An alternative inventory is in David Keirsey's *The Sixteen Types* (Del Mar: Prometheus Nemesis Book Co. 1998).

- If there is alcohol addiction in the family: Al-Anon Family Group Headquarters, Inc., 1600 Corporate Landing Parkway, Virginia Beach, VA 23454. Telephone 757-563-1600.

- Wayne Kritsberg, *The Adult Children of Alcoholics Syndrome* (New York: Bantam Books, 1985).

Bibliography

Abbot, Walter M., ed. *The Documents of Vatican II.* New York: American Press, 1966.

Achtemeier, Elizabeth. *The Committed Marriage.* Philadelphia: Westminster Press, 1976.

Barry, William, S.J. *Finding God in All Things.* Notre Dame, Ind.: Ave Maria Press, 1991.

_____. *Letting God Come Close—An Approach to the Ignatian Spiritual Exercises.* Chicago: Loyola Press, 2001.

_____. *God's Passionate Desire and Our Response.* Notre Dame, Ind.: Ave Maria Press, 1993.

Berends, Polly Berrien. *Whole child, whole parent.* New York: Harper's Magazine Press, First Edition, 1975.

Bockel, Franz, ed. *Theology in an Age of Renewal.* Concilium, New York: Herder & Herder, 1970.

Bausch, William J. *A New Look at the Sacraments.* Mystic, Conn.: Twenty-Third Publications, 1983.

Brown, Raymond E., and others. *Faith and the Future: Studies in Christian Eschatology.* John P. Galvin, ed., New York: Paulist Press, 1994.

Browning, Don S., ed. *From Culture Wars to Common Ground. Religion and the American Family Debate.* The Family, Religion, and Culture Series. Louisville: Westminster John Knox Press, 1997.

Browning, Don. *Marriage and Modernization: How Globalization Threatens Marriage and What to Do About It.* Grand Rapids: William B. Eerdmans Publishing Co., 2003.

Cahill, Lisa Sowle. *Between the Sexes: Foundations for a Christian Ethics of Sexuality.* Philadelphia: Fortress Press, 1985.

_____. *Women and Sexuality,* 1992 Madeleva Lecture in Spirituality. New York: Paulist Press, 1992.

Callahan, Sidney. *A Retreat with Mary of Magdala and Augustine, Rejoicing in Human Sexuality.* Gloria Hutchinson, ed., Cincinnati: St. Anthony Press, 1991.

Cooke, Bernard. *Ministry to Word and Sacraments.* Philadelphia: Fortress Press, 1976.

_____. *Sacraments and Sacramentality.* Mystic, Conn.: Twenty-Third Publications, 1983.

Cooke, Bernard, ed. *Alternative Futures for Worship: Vol. 5, Christian Marriage.* Collegeville: Liturgical Press, 1987.

Curtis, Brent, and John Eldredge. *The Sacred Romance:Drawing Closer to the Heart of God.* Nashville: Thomas Nelson, 1997.

Doherty, William J. *Take Back Your Marriage: Sticking Together in a World That Pulls Us Apart.* New York: Guilford Press, 2003.

Dominian, Jack. *Christian Marriage: The Challenge of Change.* London: Darton, Longman & Todd, 1967.

_____. *Dynamics of Marriage: Love, Sex and Growth from a Christian Perspective.* Mystic, Conn.: Twenty-Third Publications, 1994.

Dym, Barry. *Couples: Exploring and Understanding the Cycles of Intimate Relationships.* New York: HarperCollins, 1993.

Fox, Thomas C. *Sexuality and the Catholic Church.* New York: George Braziller, 1995.

Gottman, John. *Why Marriages Succeed or Fail, and How You Can Make Yours Last.* New York: Simon & Schuster, 1994.

_____. *The Seven Principles for Making Marriage Work.* New York: Three Rivers Press, 2000.

Heskin, Kathy. *Marriage: a Spiritual Journey.* Mystic, Conn.: Twenty-Third Publications, 2001.

Hunter, David G., ed. *Sources of Early Christian Thought: Marriage in the Early Church.* Minneapolis: Fortress Press, 1992.

John Paul II. *The Theology of the Body: Human Love in the Divine Plan.* Boston: Daughters of St. Paul, 1997.

_____. *Original Unity of Man and Woman: Catechesis on the Book of Genesis.* Boston: Daughters of St. Paul, 1981.

_____. *Familiaris Consortio.* Boston: Daughters of St. Paul, 1981.

Kasper, Walter. *Theology of Christian Marriage.* New York: Crossroad/Herder & Herder, 1980.

Kroeger, Otto, and Janet M. Thuesen. *16 Ways to Love Your Lover.* New York: Delacorte Press, 1994.

Lawler, Michael G. *Secular Marriage, Christian Sacrament.* Mystic, Conn.: Twenty-Third Publications, 1990.

———. *Marriage and Sacrament, A Theology of Christian Marriage.* Collegeville: The Liturgical Press, 1993.

Mackin, Theodore. *The Marital Sacrament.* Mahwah, N.J.: Paulist Press, 1989.

———. *What Is Marriage: Marriage in the Catholic Church.* New York: Paulist Press, 1982.

Martin, Thomas. *The Challenge of Christian Marriage.* Mahwah, N.J.: Paulist Press, 1990.

Moore, Gareth, O.P. *The Body in Context: Sex and Catholicism.* New York: Continuum, 1992.

Moore, Thomas. *Soul Mates: Honoring the Mysteries of Love and Relationship.* New York: HarperCollins, 1994.

———. *The Soul of Sex, Cultivating Life as an Act of Love.* New York: HarperCollins, 1998.

Muller, Wayne. *Sabbath: Finding Rest, Renewal, and Delight in Our Busy Lives.* New York: Random House Bantam Books, 1999.

Nelson, James B., and Sandra P. Longfellow. *Sexuality and the Sacred, Sources for Theological Reflection.* Louisville: Westminster John Knox Press, 1994.

Nouwen, Henri J. M. *The Return of The Prodigal Son.* New York: Doubleday, 1992.

Oliver, Mary Anne McPherson. *Conjugal Spirituality: The Primacy of Mutual Love in the Christian Tradition.* Kansas City, Mo.: Sheed and Ward, 1994.

Rahner, Karl. *Theological Investigations. Vol. X.* New York: Herder & Herder, 1973.

Roberts, William, ed. *Commitment to Partnership, Explorations for the Theology of Marriage.* Mahwah: Paulist Press, 1987.

———*Marriage: Sacrament of Hope and Challenge.* Cincinnati: St. Anthony Messenger Press, 1988.

Schillebeeckx, Edward. *Marriage, Human Reality and Saving Mystery.* New York: Sheed and Ward, 1965.

Scott, Kieran, and Michael Warren, eds. *Perspectives in Marriage, A Reader.* New York: Oxford University Press, 1993.

Sheldrake, Philip. *Befriending Our Desires.* Ottawa: Novalis, 2001.

Thomas, David. *Christian Marriage: A Journey Together.* Wilmington, Del.: Michael Glazier, 1983.

Timmerman, Joan. *Sexuality and Spiritual Growth.* New York: Crossroad, 1992.

_____. *The Mardi Gras Syndrome, Rethinking Christian Sexuality.* New York: Crossroad, 1984.

Tyrell, Thomas J. *The Adventure of Intimacy.* Mystic, Conn.: Twenty-Third Publications, 1994.

_____. *Urgent Longings.* Mystic, Conn.: Twenty-Third Publications, 1994.

Upton, Julia. *A Church for the Next Generation: Sacraments in Transition.* Collegeville: Liturgical Press, 1990.

Urbine, William, and William Seifert. *On Life and Love, A Guide to Catholic Teaching on Marriage and Family.* Mystic, Conn.: Twenty-Third Publications, 1996.

Westley, Dick. *Redemptive Intimacy: A New Perspective for the Journey to Adult Faith.* Mystic, Conn.: Twenty-Third Publications, 1981.